ENGLISH

Curriculum Bank

KEY STAGE ONE
SCOTTISH LEVELS A-B

WRITING

DAVID WAUGH

Published by Scholastic Ltd,
Villiers House,
Clarendon Avenue,
Leamington Spa,
Warwickshire CV32 5PR
Text © David Waugh
© 1996 Scholastic Ltd
5 6 7 8 9 0   9 0 1 2 3 4 5

AUTHOR
DAVID WAUGH

EDITOR
CLARE GALLAHER

ASSISTANT EDITOR
KATE PEARCE

SERIES DESIGNER
LYNNE JOESBURY

DESIGNER
MICKY PLEDGE

ILLUSTRATIONS
SUE KING

COVER ILLUSTRATION
GAY STURROCK

INFORMATION TECHNOLOGY CONSULTANT
MARTIN BLOWS

SCOTTISH 5–14 LINKS
MARGARET SCOTT AND SUSAN GOW

Designed using Aldus Pagemaker

British Library Cataloguing-in-Publication Data
A catalogue record for this book is available from the
British Library.

ISBN 0-590-53398-3

Contents

ACKNOWLEDGEMENTS

The author would like to thank Nick McGuinn, Head of English at Queen Margaret's School, York; Rosemary Waugh, a teacher at Kingston High School, Hull; Sally Clowe, Deputy Head of Holme-upon-Spalding-Moor Primary; Linda Darlington, Head of John Harrison C. of E., Barrow-on-Humber; Jeanette Sutherland, Deputy Head of Eastfield Primary, Hull; and the staff of Griffin Primary School for their help with ideas for this book. Thanks to Joel Lane for the text on page 157. Thanks to Mimi Everett for additional illustrations on pages 52, 53, 63, 64, 101, 107, 132 and 149.

Every effort has been made to trace copyright holders for the works reproduced in this book, and the publishers apologise for any inadvertent omissions.

Introduction

Scholastic Curriculum Bank is a series for all primary teachers, providing an essential planning tool for devising comprehensive schemes of work as well as an easily accessible and varied bank of practical, classroom-tested activities with photocopiable resources.

Designed to help planning for and implementation of progression, differentiation and assessment, *Scholastic Curriculum Bank* offers a structured range of stimulating activities with clearly stated learning objectives that reflect the programmes of study, and detailed lesson plans that allow busy teachers to put ideas into practice with the minimum amount of preparation time. The photocopiable sheets that accompany many of the activities provide ways of integrating purposeful application of knowledge and skills, differentiation, assessment and record-keeping.

Opportunities for formative assessment are highlighted within the activities where appropriate, while separate summative assessment activities give guidelines for analysis and subsequent action. Ways of using information technology for different purposes and in different contexts, as a tool for communicating and handling information and as a means of investigating, are integrated into the activities where appropriate, and more explicit guidance is provided at the end of the book.

The series covers all the primary curriculum subjects, with separate books for Key Stages 1 and 2 or Scottish Levels A–B and C–E. It can be used as a flexible resource with any scheme, to fulfil National Curriculum and Scottish 5–14 requirements and to provide children with a variety of different learning experiences that will lead to effective acquisition of skills and knowledge.

SCHOLASTIC CURRICULUM BANK ENGLISH

The *Scholastic Curriculum Bank English* books enable teachers to plan comprehensive and structured coverage of the primary English curriculum, and enable pupils to develop the required skills, knowledge and understanding through activities.

Each book contains one key stage. There are four books for Key Stage 1/Scottish levels A–B and four for Key Stage 2/Scottish levels C–E. These books reflect the English programme of study, so that there are titles on Reading, Writing, Speaking and listening and Spelling and phonics.

Bank of activities

This book provides a bank of activities which are designed to broaden children's experience of writing and enable them to develop their abilities to communicate clearly and accurately through writing.

Lesson plans

Detailed lesson plans, under clear headings, are given for each activity and provide material for immediate implementation in the classroom. The structure for each activity is as follows.

Activity title box

The information contained in the box at the beginning of each activity outlines the following key aspects:

▲ *Activity title and learning objective.* For each activity a clearly stated learning objective is given in bold italics. These learning objectives break down aspects of the programmes of study into manageable, hierarchical teaching and learning chunks, and their purpose is to aid planning for progression.

These objectives can be easily referenced to the National Curriculum and Scottish 5–14 requirements by using the overview grids at the end of this chapter (pages 9 to 14).

▲ *Class organisation/Likely duration.* Icons ✝✝ and 🕐 signpost the suggested group sizes for each activity and the approximate amount of time required to complete it.

Previous skills/knowledge needed

Information is given here when it is necessary for the children to have acquired specific knowledge or skills prior to carrying out the activity.

Key background information

The information in this section outlines the areas of study covered by each activity and gives a general background to the particular topic or theme, outlining the basic skills that will be developed and the way in which the activity will address children's learning.

Preparation

Advice is given for those occasions where it is necessary for the teacher to prime the pupils for the activity or to prepare materials, or to set up a display or activity ahead of time.

Resources needed

All of the materials needed to carry out the activity are listed, so that the pupils or the teacher can gather them together easily before the beginning of the teaching session.

What to do

Easy-to-follow, step-by-step instructions are given for carrying out the activity, including (where appropriate) suggested questions for the teacher to ask pupils to help instigate discussion and stimulate investigation.

Suggestion(s) for extension/support

Ideas are given for ways of providing easy differentiation where activities lend themselves to this purpose. In all cases, suggestions are provided as to ways in which each activity can be modified for less able or extended for more able children.

Assessment opportunities

Where appropriate, opportunities for ongoing teacher assessment of the children's work during or after a specific activity are highlighted.

Opportunities for IT

Where opportunities for IT present themselves, these are briefly outlined with reference to particularly suitable types of program. The chart on page 159 presents specific areas of IT covered in the activities, together with more detailed support on how to apply particular types of program. Selected lesson plans serve as models for other activities by providing more comprehensive guidance on the application of IT, and these are indicated by the bold page numbers on the grid and the icon at the start of an activity.

Display ideas

Where they are relevant and innovative, display ideas are incorporated into activity plans and illustrated with examples.

Other aspects of the English PoS covered

Inevitably, as all areas of English are interrelated, activities will cover aspects of the programmes of study in other areas of the English curriculum. These links are highlighted under this heading.

Reference to photocopiable sheets

Where activities include photocopiable activity sheets, small reproductions of these are included in the lesson plans together with guidance notes for their use and, where appropriate, suggested answers.

Assessment

In this book, advice is given for each activity on what the teacher should look out for during the course of the activity. Notes made on individual children's progress may contribute to an overall profile of each child which could include samples of writing in various genres.

At the end of each chapter there is an activity which is designed to provide a summative measure of a range of key competencies linked to the type of writing dealt with in that chapter. This activity is similar in its organisation to the preceding ones, and focuses on a number of learning objectives covered in the chapter. Assessment activities are indicated by the icon.

Photocopiable activity sheets

Many of the activities are accompanied by photocopiable activity sheets. For some activities, there may be more than one version; or an activity sheet may be 'generic', with a facility for the teacher to fill in the appropriate task in order to provide differentiation by task. Other sheets may be more open-ended to provide differentiation by outcome. The photocopiable activity sheets provide purposeful activities that are ideal for assessment and can be kept as records in pupils' portfolios of work.

Cross-curricular links

Cross-curricular links are identified on a simple grid which cross-references the particular areas of study in English to the programmes of study for other subjects in the curriculum, and where appropriate provides suggestions for activities (see page 160).

WRITING

This book is intended to help teachers to fulfil the National Curriculum requirement that at Key Stage 1 children 'should be helped to understand the value of writing as a means of remembering, communicating, organising and developing ideas and information, and as a source of enjoyment'.

Children's views of writing are often formulated during their early years in school. It is, therefore, vital that they should come to regard writing as a pleasurable and purposeful activity. Donald Graves maintained: 'Children want to write. They want to write the first day they attend school. This is no accident. Before they went to school they marked up walls, pavements, newspapers with crayons, chalk, pens or pencils... anything that makes a mark.' (*Writing: Teachers and Children at Work* by D. Graves, Heinemann, 1983). It is surely one of our most important duties as educators to ensure that this early enthusiasm is built upon, nurtured and developed.

The activities in this book are designed to allow children to develop their skills as writers through challenging and meaningful work. There is an emphasis upon writing for real audiences which might include adults, other children and, sometimes, the author herself.

Nigel Hall, in his introduction to *Writing with Reason* (Hodder & Stoughton, 1989), asked why so many reports and surveys 'reveal young children doing little more than repetitious, low level skill activities as the major part, and in many cases the totality, of their writing experiences'. It is hoped that this book offers a variety of activities which will allow children to practise their writing skills in a meaningful way. The activities range from listing and labelling to simple sentence writing, and from letter writing to creating stories and poems. Some of the activities involve writing to communicate with real or imaginary audiences. There are also activities which might be attempted as part of a theme on birthdays, Christmas or shopping.

Children's writing will develop best when they are exposed to a range of literature which will provide them with ideas about style and content. The book includes many references to stories and poems which the children might read or hear as a prelude to independent writing.

The language study section of the book is intended to develop children's awareness of written English and the possibilities which are available to them. For example, there are several activities designed to encourage the use of adverbs and adjectives, as well as others which highlight the ways in which words may be used to provide information.

The most important aim of the book is to make children feel that they want to write and to offer a diversity of activities which will afford them the opportunity to do so successfully.

Learning objective	PoS/AO	Content	Type of activity	Page
Language study				
To show an ability to form letters with increasing accuracy.	1a; 2e. *Handwriting and presentation: Level A.*	Talking about letters and various finger-writing activities to develop letter formation.	Individuals writing letters and finding letters to trace over.	16
To demonstrate increased ability to discriminate between letters and to write names. To develop letter formation.	1a; 2e. *As above.*	Discussing families and looking at relevant words.	Individuals drawing pictures and writing names of family members.	17
To demonstrate an ability to write names and appreciate the function of print through the production of a book about themselves.	1a; 2a. *Personal writing: Level A. Handwriting: Level A.*	Collecting and discussing photographs.	Individuals making a book about themselves with adult help.	18
To look closely at names and copy them accurately.	1a; 2a. *As above.*	Discussing pictures of members of the class as babies.	Individuals or pairs looking at photographs and writing names to match.	19
To write names accurately, using capital letters for the beginning of the name.	1a; 2c. *Functional writing: Level A.*	Discussing pictures of people and deciding upon names for them.	Individuals or pairs looking at the photocopiable sheet and writing names for the people on the bus.	20
To show increased awareness of the written form.	1a; 2a. *Personal writing: Level A.*	Discussing writing with individuals or pairs.	Individuals or pairs working with an adult to write a conversation.	21
To show increased knowledge of colours and spell their names correctly.	1a; 2d. *Spelling: Level A.*	Discussing colours of different items around the classroom and the spelling of their names.	Children using the photocopiable sheet individually or in pairs to match colours to items.	21
To demonstrate an ability to write in sentences and to spell simple and common words.	1a; 2c, d; 3a. *Spelling: Level A. Structure: Level A.*	Discussing names and spellings of items of clothing.	Individuals or pairs writing sentences in response to photocopiable sheet.	23
To show an ability to complete sentences.	1a; 2c; 3a. *Punctuation and structure: Level A. Spelling: Level A.*	Discussing houses and streets and the way in which names are written.	Individuals or pairs writing sentences in response to photocopiable sheet.	24
To be able to write in sentences and to use capital letters and full stops appropriately.	1a; 2c. *Punctuation and structure: Level A.*	Discussing pets and pet ownership.	Individuals or pairs writing sentences in response to photocopiable sheet.	25
To demonstrate developing letter formation skills and clear and neat presentation.	1a; 2e. *Handwriting and presentation: Level A.*	Examining packaging of products and discussing its qualities.	Individuals or pairs designing packaging and writing on labels.	26
To demonstrate increasing knowledge of sound–symbol correspondence and phonological patterns.	1a; 2d. *Spelling: Level A.*	Looking at sound cards and trying to find words in a passage of prose which contain the sounds.	Small groups or pairs using books and sound cards to help them compile a list of words.	27
To produce writing based upon close reading of words which are found in the classroom.	1a; 2d. *Functional writing: Level A.*	Looking at names of items to be found around the classroom.	Small groups writing sentences describing where different items are kept.	28
To produce simple writing and sentence writing.	1a; 2c. *Punctuation and structure: Level A.*	Discussing people who help us.	Individuals or pairs writing sentences explaining how people help them.	29

Learning objective	PoS/AO	Content	Type of activity	Page
To be able to use question marks and to write sentences.	1a; 2c; 3a. *Punctuation and structure: Level C.*	Discussing a forthcoming topic for study.	Pairs or small groups composing questions about a topic to be studied.	30
To use capital letters accurately and to be able to explain their usage.	1a; 2c. *Punctuation and structure: Level A.*	Studying the use of capital letters.	Whole-class discussion followed by individual or paired work identifying words which require capital letters.	31
To demonstrate understanding of the ways in which phrases and clauses can link together to make sentences.	1a; 2c; 3a. *Punctuation and structure: Level B.*	Combining phrases and clauses to make sentences.	Whole-class discussion followed by individual or paired writing.	33
To demonstrate a developing understanding of the use of commas to separate words in lists.	1a; 2c; 3a. *Punctuation and structure: Level C.*	Discussing the use of commas.	Whole-class discussion followed by individual or paired written work.	34
To demonstrate an increased knowledge of common prefixes and suffixes.	1a; 2d. *Spelling: Level B.*	Discussion about words beginning with un- and words ending with -ing.	Groups working together to find as many words with un- at the beginning or -ing at the end as possible.	36
To use imaginative vocabulary choices and to demonstrate an awareness of adjectives and their function.	1a; 2b. *Knowledge about language: Level B.*	Discussion about the word 'nice' and alternatives to it.	Individuals using the photocopiable sheet as a stimulus to find alternatives to the word 'nice'.	37
To demonstrate an increased understanding of the importance of correct word order in sentences.	1a; 3a. *As above.*	Looking at jumbled sentences and determining correct word order.	Individuals and pairs writing jumbled messages for translation.	38
To demonstrate increased awareness of the features of different types of writing.	1a b, c. *Awareness of genre: Level B.*	Discussing collections of writing made by the children and teacher.	Individuals writing descriptions of the different types of writing in their collections.	39
To demonstrate understanding of opposites and an ability to use sentence writing within a structured activity.	1a; 3b. *Knowledge about language: Level B.*	Discussing antonyms with the whole group.	Pairs writing sentences with opposite meanings to those on the photocopiable sheet.	40
To show increased knowledge of words and their meanings and improved spelling of common homonyms.	1a; 3b. *Spelling: Level B.*	Discussing common homonyms and making a collection.	Children making collections of homonyms both in and out of school.	41
To understand the function of adverbs and to produce descriptive and poetic writing.	1a, c; 3b. *Knowledge about language: Level B.*	Discussing the function of adverbs.	Individuals using photographs of animals as a stimulus to writing adverb poems.	42
To demonstrate an understanding of the concept of subject–verb agreement in writing.	1a, c; 3a. *Knowledge about language: Level D.*	Discussing young children's language.	Using the photocopiable sheet to translate young child's errors into standard English.	44
To write a story with a clear beginning, middle and end, demonstrating the ability to use appropriate punctuation, spelling and presentational skills.	1a, b, c; 2a, b, c; 3a, b. *Punctuation and structure: Level C. Spelling: Level C.*	Listening to and discussing a story.	Children writing stories individually.	45

Learning objective	PoS/AO	Content	Type of activity	Page
Imaginative writing				
To make use of adjectives in descriptive writing.	1a; 3b. *Imaginative writing: Level B.*	Discussing pictures of people and ways of describing them.	Children writing sentences using adjectives to describe people.	48
To make use of adjectives to describe the feel and appearance of different materials.	1a, b; 3a. *As above.*	Children feel different objects and describe them.	Writing descriptions individually or in pairs.	49
To present ideas imaginatively without writing sentences and to use these as a basis for poetry or prose writing.	1a; 3b. *Imaginative writing: Level A.*	Discussing synonyms and making a class chart.	Children working individually or in pairs to make happy charts.	50
To write in response to a stimulus, showing an ability to use a prayer format.	1a, c. *Personal writing: Level B.*	Discussing harvest-time and reasons for being grateful for foods we eat.	Children working in groups to write harvest prayers.	51
To write a letter for a 'real' audience.	1a, b. *Functional writing: Level B.*	Discussing Christmas presents which children would like family and friends to receive.	Individual children writing letters to Santa Claus.	52
To produce descriptive and commentary writing.	1a; 2b. *Imaginative writing: Level B.*	Discussing real and imaginary monsters and their characteristics.	Pairs or individuals drawing and writing descriptions of imaginary monsters.	54
To use captions and descriptive writing.	1a; 3a. *Functional writing: Level A.*	Reading about and discussing fantastic machines.	Individuals or pairs designing and labelling machines.	55
To produce note-making and sentence writing in an imaginative piece of writing.	1a, c. *Imaginative writing: Level B.*	Discussing and making a scarecrow.	Individuals or pairs writing from the point of view of a scarecrow.	55
To demonstrate a growing awareness of sound–symbol relationships and phonological patterns through an imaginative writing activity.	1a; 2d. *As above.*	Reading and discussing tongue-twisters.	Individuals or pairs writing tongue-twisters.	57
To produce writing in response to a stimulus.	1a, b. *As above.*	Looking at and discussing famous paintings.	Paired writing of descriptions of famous pictures.	58
To organise and plan writing through analysis of a well-known story.	1a; 2b. *As above.*	Reading and discussing well-known stories.	Individuals or pairs writing about key events in a story.	58
To produce narrative writing in response to listening to a story related to an educational visit.	1a, c. *As above.*	Listening to a story about a school visit and discussing ways of continuing the story.	Individuals continuing the teacher's story in writing.	59
To write a story in response to a stimulus.	1a, b. *As above.*	Looking at a map of a fantasy island and discussing its features.	Children continuing, individually or in pairs, a story about a visit to an island.	60
To write imaginatively in response to a stimulus.	1a, c. *As above.*	Reading and discussing stories with three wishes theme.	Individuals or pairs responding to story on photocopiable sheet and then continuing it.	62
To plan a story and to write in sentences through an activity based upon a published story.	1a; 2b. *As above.*	Discussing stories and the ability to change.	Individuals planning and writing stories about changing their lives.	63

Learning objective	PoS/AO	Content	Type of activity	Page
To produce imaginative, chronological writing in timetable form.	1a, c. *Imaginative writing: Level B.*	Discussing ideal birthdays.	Children working individually to write timetables for their ideal birthdays.	64
To write for a purpose in response to the stimulus provided by reading a story.	1a, b. *Personal writing: Level A.*	Discussing a story and the example of a game related to the story provided on the photocopiable sheet.	Children working in pairs or small groups to plan and make a game based upon a story which they know or have read.	65
To demonstrate an increased awareness of and ability to use the characteristics of narrative writing.	1a, c; 2b. *Imaginative writing: Level B.*	Studying story structure and the characteristics of narrative writing.	Whole-class discussion followed by individuals or pairs writing the middle section of the story on the photocopiable sheet.	67
To produce narrative writing which involves continuing and completing a story.	1a, c. *As above.*	Reading and discussing story provided on the photocopiable sheet.	Individuals or pairs planning and writing a continuation of the story on the photocopiable sheet.	68
To interact with texts and to write endings for stories.	1a, c; 3a. *As above.*	Studying story structure and the characteristics of narrative writing.	Whole-class discussion followed by individuals or pairs placing sentences in correct order to make a story. Writing an ending for the story.	69
To produce descriptive writing based upon planning and note-making.	1a; 2b. *Functional writing: Level B.*	Listening to and reading descriptions of everyday things.	Individuals making notes and then writing sentences to describe everyday things.	71
To produce narrative writing which is planned and drafted in response to a stimulus.	1a, b. *Imaginative writing: Level B.*	Reading and discussing stories about little people.	Individuals or pairs writing stories about being very small.	72
To produce descriptive writing based on a familiar stimulus.	1a, c. *Personal writing: Level B.*	Discussing favourite toys and reasons for liking them.	Individuals or pairs writing about favourite toys.	73
To produce narrative writing in cartoon form with a clearly defined beginning, middle and end.	1a; 2a. *Imaginative writing: Level B.*	Discussing and looking at favourite toys and reading a story about a lost toy.	Individuals or pairs planning and writing story using pictures and text.	74
To write and show an appreciation of pattern in poetry.	1a; 2b. *As above.*	Reading poems and discussing repetitive patterns.	Individuals writing repetitive poems.	75
To plan and review writing and to use imaginative vocabulary.	1a; 2b. *As above.*	Listening to poems about the weather and discussing descriptions.	Individuals or pairs planning and writing weather poems.	76
To produce descriptive writing using notes.	1a; 2b. *Functional writing: Level A.*	Examining leaves closely and describing them.	Individual descriptions of leaves.	77
To write imaginatively after drawing.	1a, c. *Functional writing: Level B.*	Discussing features of imaginary cars as seen in films or described in literature.	Individuals or pairs drawing and writing descriptions of ideal cars.	78
To use knowledge of sound–symbol correspondence to write acrostics, using sentences.	1a, c. *Imaginative writing: Level B.*	Class work creating acrostics.	Individuals or pairs writing acrostics.	79

Overview grid

Learning objective	PoS/AO	Content	Type of activity	Page
To produce list writing and imaginative writing.	1a, b *Functional writing: Level B.*	Movement work involving mime.	Individuals or pairs making notes and then writing sentences about the seaside.	80
To produce chronological story writing in response to a stimulus.	1a, b. *Imaginative writing: Level B.*	Class discussion of picture stories.	Individuals or pairs writing sentences to describe the events in a picture story.	81
To make choices about vocabulary and to produce collaborative writing.	1a, c. *As above.*	Listening to and describing sounds and making recordings of sounds around the school.	Pairs writing short poems describing sounds heard around the school.	82
To develop the ability to write imaginatively and with confidence, fluency and accuracy in response to a stimulus.	1a, b, c; 2a, b, c. *Imaginative writing: Level B.*	Listening to and discussing beginning of a story.	Children writing stories individually.	83
Non-fiction writing				
To convey a message in a visual form by producing well-presented posters.	1a, b; 2e. *Handwriting and presentation: Level B.*	Discussing strangers and the danger of going with them.	Individuals or pairs planning and producing posters.	86
To record ideas in a diagrammatic form.	1a, c. *As above.*	Discussing things which we use our hands to do.	Individuals or pairs making charts showing the uses of hands.	87
To copy words accurately and to label clearly.	1a, c; 2e. *Functional writing: Level B.*	Discussing presents appropriate for a Christmas stocking.	Individuals cutting out Christmas stockings and pictures of presents and then labelling them.	87
To make simple notes as aidé-memoires.	1a, b. *Functional writing: Level A.*	Playing the game 'I went on my holiday' orally.	Individuals making notes on photocopiable sheet to help them to remember items taken on holiday.	88
To present writing carefully for an audience.	1a, b; 2e. *Handwriting and presentation: Level A.*	Discussing examples of signs found in the environment and the importance of careful presentation.	Individuals or pairs planning and making signs for the classroom and/or the school.	89
To make accurate use of simple words and phrases.	1a, c. *Functional writing: Level A.*	Discussing shopping lists and the contents of the class shop.	Individuals or pairs writing shopping lists.	90
To write for an audience in a concise and eye-catching way.	1a; 2e. *Handwriting and presentation: Level A.*	Examining packaging and advertisements.	Individuals or pairs making posters to advertise products in the class or school shop.	91
To use a range of reading and writing skills in an ongoing activity and to be aware of the communicative nature of writing.	1a, c. *Personal writing: Level A.*	Discovery of a 'visitor' and letters from the 'visitor' and discussion.	Children working collectively and then individually or in pairs to respond to the visitor's letters.	92
To label and copy words accurately.	1a, c. *Functional writing: Level A.*	Discussion of a story about a bicycle and examination of a real bicycle.	Individuals or pairs labelling picture of bicycle provided on photocopiable sheet.	93
To present accurate descriptive writing for an audience.	1a, b. *Functional writing: Level B.*	Examination of a bicycle and discussion of ways of describing it.	Individuals or pairs writing descriptions of a bicycle to enable identification.	95

Learning objective	PoS/AO	Content	Type of activity	Page
To write accurately for an audience and to make use of knowledge of sound–symbol correspondence.	1a, b; 3b. Functional writing: Level B.	Children look at and discuss lists.	Whole-class discussion followed by completing and creating lists individually or in pairs.	96
To write in sentences and use recording skills.	1a; 2c. Personal writing: Level B.	Discussion of things which happen during the school day.	Individuals or pairs recording events during the day in sentences.	97
To write for an audience, showing awareness of the spellings of classmates' names and making use of presentational skills.	1a, b. Functional writing: Level B. Handwriting and presentation: Level B.	Discussion about birthday parties.	Individuals or pairs making lists and preparing invitations.	98
To write instructions using complete sentences with capital letters and full stops and to develop chronological writing.	1a, c; 3a. Functional writing: Level B.	Playing and discussing party games.	Pairs writing instructions for party games.	99
To use lists and to organise work and present it in conjunction with pictures.	1a, c; 2e. Functional writing: Level A.	Discussing parties and party food.	Individuals or pairs making lists of party foods and adding pictures.	100
To write for an audience using features of presentation.	1a, b; 2e. Handwriting and presentation: Level B.	Looking at examples of birthday cards and discussing them.	Individuals or pairs making birthday cards for family or friends.	101
To write accurately using commonly used words and/or words which are needed for a topic.	1a; 2d. Spelling: Level A/B.	Discussing spellings and alphabetical order.	Whole class or group writing words on card or paper or in books to create a word bank.	102
To write for an audience.	1a, b. Functional writing: Level B.	Discussing treasure hunts and children taking part in one.	Pairs or individuals devising and writing treasure-hunt clues.	103
To use a format for letter writing and to write for an audience.	1a, c. Personal writing: Level B.	Reading letters and discussing their structure and possible content.	Individuals writing letters to their parents about what they do at school.	105
To use letter writing for a real audience.	1a, b. As above.	Discussing pen-pals and the things one would want to tell them and find out about them.	Individuals or pairs writing letters to pen-pals.	106
To produce independent writing in response to a discussion about a familiar institution.	1a, b, c. As above.	Discussing the meaning of Christmas and listening to a recording.	Individuals or pairs explaining about Christmas and writing about what it means to them.	107
To write about personal experiences and to organise writing appropriately.	1a, b, c; 2a, b, c. Personal writing: Level B.	Discussing memories of first days at school.	Children writing individually about their first day at school.	108

Entries given in italics relate to the Scottish 5–14 Guidelines for English Language.

Language study

In this chapter activities are provided which are designed to raise children's awareness of the ways in which language may be used in writing. As they develop as writers, children will benefit from possessing greater knowledge of the ways in which authors use devices such as punctuation in order to help them to convey meaning.

Children meet language in a variety of forms and this section is intended to allow them to experience many of those forms which are relevant to their age and experience. Labelling and the making of lists are key elements in early writing and there are opportunities to develop these styles of presentation in this section. Many of the activities involve the development of basic skills in writing, but these are based upon oral work and reading rather than taking the form of traditional grammar exercises. Where exercises are provided, they are designed to help teachers to assess children's progress and to reinforce knowledge rather than as devices for teaching skills.

In addition, there are activities designed to foster co-operative writing with other children and with more experienced writers. Children are provided with opportunities to discuss their writing and to share and compare ideas and should not always perceive writing as a solitary activity. It is through this co-operation and the provision of real audiences for their writing that they should become increasingly aware of the possibilities for communication which an ability to write confidently, fluently and accurately affords.

LETTER PATTERNS

To show an ability to form letters with increasing accuracy.

†† *Children who need help with recognising and writing letters working individually.*

🕐 *30–40 minutes.*

Previous skills/knowledge needed
Children will need some basic knowledge of letters and the ways in which they are formed.

Key background information
In this activity children are asked to write individual letters to form patterns on paper. Particular attention is given to correct letter formation. The activity also provides an opportunity to examine abilities to hold pencils correctly. It is important that children learn to form letters correctly at an early stage before bad habits are internalised, causing problems in later cursive writing.

Preparation
Prepare A4 sheets with letters written in a large size on them. Make letters out of felt material, and draw letters lightly in pencil, on A4 sheets of paper, for those children who may need outlines of letters to follow.

Resources needed
Letter sheets (see above), felt letters, plain A4 paper, sand trays, broad felt-tipped pens, writing pencils. For support activity – A4 sheets on which there are letters drawn in pencil.

What to do
Focus on one letter at a time. Begin the activity by letting the children write letters with their fingers. They can do this in the air or in sand trays (which can be made by putting a thin layer of sand into a biscuit-tin lid). The children can also trace over felt letters with their fingers. It is important to show the children where the letters should begin and end, and to stress the correct formation through tactile activities.

The children can go on to use pencils or broad felt-tipped pens to draw letters on plain paper. When the children have become familiar with the writing of a letter and have practised writing it, give them a piece of paper with the letter written in a large size on it. Ask them to fill the space inside or around the letter with lots of similar letters.

The children could go on to write other letters, or could look at a piece of writing and try to find as many examples of particular letters as possible and trace over them with a felt-tipped pen.

Suggestion(s) for extension
The main activity is designed for children who are just beginning to write. Those who are more advanced could focus

upon groups of common letter strings and families of letters. Common groupings are as follows:

Anti-clockwise letters
a c d e g o q
Clockwise letters
b p
Hump Letters
h m n r
Trough letters
u v w y
Line letters
f i j k l t z
Irregular letters
s x

The children could practise writing words with letter strings such as 'ing', 'ion' and 'ed'.

Suggestion(s) for support
It may be necessary for some children to trace letters until their confidence in letter formation and pencil manipulation grows. Using broad felt-tipped pens, the children can draw over the letters that you have already drawn in pencil.

Assessment opportunities
Look for evidence that children are holding pencils correctly with a tripod grip (between thumb and index finger supported by middle finger) and are able to form letters correctly, starting and finishing in the correct places.

Display ideas
Displays of children's letter patterns could be accompanied by examples of adult writing and printing and, perhaps, writing by older children which shows what the younger ones will be progressing towards.

Other aspects of the English PoS covered
Reading – 2b.

MY FAMILY

To demonstrate increased ability to discriminate between letters and to write names. To develop letter formation.

†† *Whole class or group, working individually.*

🕐 *One hour.*

Key background information

In this activity the children draw a picture of their family and label it. The topic will need to be treated with sensitivity because some children do not come from families in which a mother and father live at home. However, the work might be linked to personal, social and moral education.

The activity requires children to label pictures with names, but many children may be able to go on to write sentences about members of their family, possibly with the aid of *Breakthrough to Literacy* materials (David Mackay *et al.*, Longman) or similar word cards which will enable them physically to manipulate text.

Preparation

The children could be asked to bring to school photographs of their family so that they can use these as aids to drawing pictures. If this is not possible, they can draw pictures without them. Write 'family' words on small pieces of card for the children to refer to.

Resources needed

Photographs of members of your own family, photographs of children's families, chalkboard, pieces of card, writing materials. *Breakthrough to Literacy* materials (by David Mackay *et al.*, Longman) – optional.

What to do

Talk with the children about families and ask them to talk about the people in their family. Write words such as 'Mummy', 'Daddy', 'brother' and 'sister' on the board and on pieces of card so that children can become familiar with them and perhaps use them in their later writing. Tell the children about your own family and show them your photographs.

Ask the children to draw pictures of the members of their family and to name each person whom they draw. Help them with the writing of names and use the opportunity to talk about letter sounds. Where names have alternative spellings (Steven/Stephen, Jill/Gill, Clare/Claire and so on) children's attention may be drawn to the fact that the same sound can sometimes be made by different letters.

Suggestion(s) for extension

Some children may go on to write sentences about their family which may range from the simple 'I like my Mummy' to 'My Mummy works at...' Beginnings of sentences could be provided for the children to complete and a word bank made available to help them. *Breakthrough to Literacy* materials (David Mackay *et al.*, Longman), if available, may be useful here.

Suggestion(s) for support

Some children may need help in writing the names of the members of their family. You could write them faintly for the child to trace over or the children could be given individual cards to match to their pictures before copying the words.

Assessment opportunities

Look for evidence of children being able to copy letters and words accurately and note their successes in forming letters correctly.

Opportunities for IT

The children could use a concept keyboard attached to a computer. The concept keyboard overlay could contain a range of suitable words which will appear on the screen when pressed. The children could type other words at the keyboard, or be helped to do so by another adult. A similar activity could be undertaken with framework software like *My World 2*.

Display ideas

Pictures and writing could be displayed, together with a picture and some writing about your own family.

Other aspects of the English PoS covered

Speaking and listening – 1a, b.
Reading – 2b.

WRITING YOUR NAME

To demonstrate an ability to write names and appreciate the function of print through the production of a book about themselves.

†† *Individuals with help from adults.*

🕐 *Work done over a period of time.*

Previous skills/knowledge needed

The children will need to have knowledge of the conventions of reading a book.

Key background information

In this activity the children make a book about themselves. The book is written with a great deal of help from adults, but the child has repeated opportunities to write his or her name. Many children arrive at school able to write their names but very little else. This can be a starting point for both reading and writing as the children begin to see that other words can be written to represent things which they can see and touch.

Preparation

Read with the children books about other children. If possible, bring in a copy of a book which has the name of a member of the class as a central character. It is possible to buy books which include a chosen name in the story.

Ask each child to think about what he or she would like in his or her book. Take a photograph of each child and/or ask the children to bring in photographs from home. (If children

are asking their parents for photographs, it would be a good idea to send a letter home, explaining why these are needed.)

Prepare name cards for children needing support work.

Resources needed

Story books about children, camera, collections of photographs from home, A4 paper, writing pencils. Card for support activity.

What to do

Using the photographs, work with the children to make books in which they are the central characters. The books may be stories or they may be biographical. Write for the children where necessary, but leave blank spaces for the child's name. The child will fill in the spaces. Each page of writing can be done on a loose sheet and later put into a book, or a booklet of perhaps eight pages could be made by folding A4 plain paper and stapling it together.

It is important at all stages in the writing of the books to discuss the letters and the words and to help each child to form letters and hold a pencil correctly.

When the books have been completed, ask the children to read them to each other and to the class. Some children may not be able to read the words literally, without adult help, but they should be assisted to become familiar with the text, so that they may talk about what is written. Books can be sent home for parents to see and then placed in the class library.

Suggestion(s) for extension

Some children may be capable of more independent work, and may write simple sentences for their books to describe the actions in the photographs.

Suggestion(s) for support

Provide name cards for children to copy in order to encourage a degree of independence from the adult helper.

Assessment opportunities

Look at the books to assess accuracy of name spelling and observe children's pencil holding and letter formation.

Opportunities for IT

Those children already adept at forming letters could use a word processor, a concept keyboard or software such as *My World 2* for their writing.

Display ideas

Cover the books with self-adhesive plastic film and display, before placing them in the class library.

Other aspects of the English PoS covered

Speaking and listening – 1a.
Reading – 1a.

BABIES

To look closely at names and copy them accurately.

†† *Whole class or group, working individually or in pairs.*

🕐 *Children take turns to do the activity over a period of, perhaps, one day.*

Key background information
In this activity the children each bring to school a photograph of themselves as babies. These are displayed and the children have to look at them carefully and write down whom they think each photograph shows. The use of personal photographs sets the activity within the child's experiences, as does the use of names of children within the class.

Preparation
Send a letter to parents asking them if they could provide a photograph of their child as a baby. Prepare a list of the children's names in the class, look at it with the children and ask them to read it.

photographs of them as babies on the wall, and that they will be able to take turns to look at the display and try to identify the babies. Place the class list next to the photographs, so that the children can copy names accurately.

Give the children a sheet of paper with numbers for each photograph down the left-hand side. Let the children try to write the name of the person whom they think is shown in each photograph next to the appropriate number.

Suggestion(s) for extension
Children could write a sentence for each picture, explaining why they have identified it as being of a particular person.

Suggestion(s) for support
Children may work in pairs for mutual support.

Assessment opportunities
Note the children's abilities to write names accurately. Note, too, their use of capital letters when appropriate.

Resources needed
General pictures of babies, photographs of famous people as babies (optional), photographs of the children in the class as babies, a class list of the children's names, writing materials.

What to do
Show the children pictures of babies. It may be possible to make a collection of pictures of famous people as babies to show to the children.

Talk with the children about the ways in which we change as we grow older. Show them a photograph of you and/or your family as babies. Tell them that you have put the

Opportunities for IT
The children could use a word processor to write and print a label for their own photograph, giving their name and a sentence about themselves. These could then be cut out and mixed up. Each child could then pick out one label and try and attach it to the correct photograph.

Display ideas
The wall display of pictures can be a working display, which children can take turns to use.

Other aspects of the English PoS covered
Speaking and listening – 2b.

PEOPLE ON THE BUS

To write names accurately, using capital letters for the beginning of the name.

†† *Whole class or group, working individually or in pairs.*
🕐 *One hour.*

Previous skills/knowledge needed

Children will need to know that names are written with capital letters at the beginning. They may need to be introduced to abbreviated titles such as Mr, Mrs and Miss.

Key background information

In this activity children are given a picture of a bus with people on it. They then have to think of names for the people on the bus and write them down. There is emphasis placed on the use of capital letters to begin names and for titles, such as Mr and Mrs. Children could make up funny names for the people, and could use their growing knowledge of sound–symbol correspondence to do this.

Preparation

Cut pictures of people out of magazines. Make copies of photocopiable page 110, one for each child or pair. Cut off the names of the people for photocopiable sheets used in the main activity; children doing the support activity will need the whole of the sheet.

Resources needed

Pictures of people cut out of magazines, photocopiable page 110, chalkboard, writing materials. Dictionaries and telephone books for extension activity.

What to do

Draw some simple pictures of people on the board or, if you are not confident about this, cut out some pictures of people from magazines. Show the children the pictures and ask them to think of names for the people.

Give out the copies of photocopiable page 110 (without the names) and tell the children to look at the picture of the people on the bus. Ask the children to suggest names for some of the people. If the forenames are the same as those of children in the class, encourage them to go to labelled drawers, lists and so on to find spellings before writing the names on a separate sheet of paper (listing an appropriate

name against each person's number). If the names are new, write them on the board for the children. The children can work in pairs to find names if you wish.

Suggestion(s) for extension

Children might use lists of names from dictionaries or even from the telephone directory. This would also help to develop an appreciation of alphabetical order.

Suggestion(s) for support

Photocopiable page 110 has some names, including some with titles, to use for those children needing support work. Tell the children to match each name to the person to whom they think it belongs and write the names on a sheet of paper with numbers 1 to 11 down the left-hand side. It may be necessary to spend additional time with some children to help them to read the names on the photocopiable sheet. (These are all phonically regular.)

Assessment opportunities

Note the children's abilities to copy words accurately. Where children go on to make up their own names, look for signs that they are able to make use of their knowledge of sound–symbol relationships.

Opportunities for IT

Once the list of names for the people on the bus has been compiled, each child could select one name, use a word processor to write it, and then print it out.

▲ Write a name for each person on the bus.

People on the bus

Mrs Smith Tim Binns Mrs Brown Mrs Thompson James Wilson Mr Little Mrs Jones Sam King Sally Dixon Mr Harry Watson Mr Todd

Display ideas

Display an enlarged copy of the bus on photocopiable page 110, together with the children's suggested names for the driver and passengers.

Other aspects of the English PoS covered

Speaking and listening – 3b.
Reading – 2b.

Reference to photocopiable sheet

Photocopiable page 110 provides a picture of a bus with a driver and passengers and a list of possible names for them. The children use the sheet without the names for the main activity, writing names of their own choice on a separate sheet of paper. In the support activity, the children use the whole sheet, matching the names to the people.

A WRITTEN CONVERSATION

To show increased awareness of the written form.
†† *Whole class or group, working individually or in pairs.*
🕐 *One hour.*

Key background information

In this activity the child works with an adult or a more experienced writing partner to produce a piece of writing which is, effectively, a conversation written down. This provides an opportunity to show to children that it is possible to write down things which are spoken.

Preparation

Make a list of possible areas of conversation in which the children could be involved.

Resources needed

List of possible areas of conversation, writing materials. Chalkboard for extension activity. Drawing materials for support activity.

What to do

Sit next to the child if you are working with an individual. Write down, with the child watching you carefully, 'My name is...' and your name. It is important that the child does not look at the paper upside down, so he or she should sit or stand next to you. Ask the child to write 'My name is...' and his or her name. If this proves difficult, write the child's name or part of it yourself.

Next, write 'I live in...' and the town or village where you live. Ask the child to do the same, helping wherever necessary. Continue the conversation with 'I like to go to...', 'I like to eat...', 'My best friend is...' and so on.

Suggestion(s) for extension

The activity could be undertaken with a group, with you writing on the board and the children writing on paper. It is important that the group is not so large that you do not have sufficient time to observe each child closely.

Suggestion(s) for support

Where the child finds it difficult to write a word, he or she may draw a picture and then have the word written by you.

Assessment opportunities

Look closely at the child's ability to hold a pencil correctly, to write from left to right, to write his or her name, to form letters correctly, and to understand that print can convey messages.

Display ideas

Books could be produced, with the written conversations being added to regularly and pictures of the child and the person with whom the conversation is held, on the cover. The writing could then form part of the child's reading.

Other aspects of the English PoS covered

Speaking and listening – 2b.

COLOURS

To show increased knowledge of colours and spell their names correctly.
†† *Whole class or group, working individually or in pairs.*
🕐 *One hour.*

Previous skills/knowledge needed

Children will need to have some knowledge of the basic colours. Those who have very little knowledge may still attempt this activity with support.

Key background information

This activity is designed to develop children's knowledge of colours and their abilities to write the names of colours. The names of most of the common colours are phonically regular and so this activity provides an opportunity to develop and reinforce phonic awareness.

Preparation

Collect items of different colours and make accompanying cards with the names of common colours written on them. (You could write the words in the appropriate colour to help reinforce children's knowledge of colours.) Make a list of items which can be found in the classroom and photocopy it for each child or pair. Find a copy of Christina Rossetti's poem 'What is Pink?' – this is included in the *Hutchinson Treasury of Children's Literature* edited by Alison Sage

(Hutchinson, 1995) – and other poems about colours to read to the children. Photocopy page 111, one copy for each child. For the extension activity, collect paint charts made for leading manufacturers. These are easily obtainable from DIY shops. For the support activity, make or buy some flash cards showing a full range of colours.

Resources needed

The poem 'What is Pink?' (see 'Preparation'), other poems about colours, a list of items in the classroom, different-coloured items which have been labelled with their colours, photocopiable page 111, coloured sticky paper, writing materials. Paint charts for extension activity. Flash cards showing different colours (commercial ones or cards which you have made) for support activity.

What to do

Read poems to the children in which colours feature strongly. Christina Rossetti's poem 'What is Pink?' (see 'Preparation') provides a good starting point for discussing colours. Talk with the children about colours and discuss the colours of, for example, their clothes and items around the classroom. Ask about their favourite colours.

Give out copies of photocopiable page 111 and provide each child with pieces of coloured sticky paper in different colours. Ask the children to stick their pieces of coloured paper on to the boxes on the photocopiable sheet (each box is labelled with a colour) and then write a list, underneath each box, of items which are the same colours. Explain that the colours on the paper will not correspond exactly to the colours of the items. The children can use the list of items which you have prepared (showing items found around the classroom) to help them with the writing of the words. They

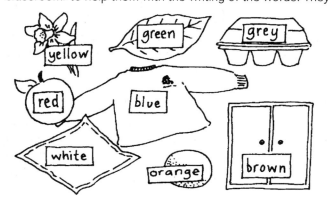

can also refer to the various items that you have collected and labelled with a range of colours.

A discussion of the different *shades* of colours would be fruitful. Some children may be encouraged to add words to the items on their list to make phrases such as 'dark green board' or 'light blue cloth'.

Suggestion(s) for extension

Provide the children with colour charts produced by paint manufacturers and ask them how closely they can match these to items in the classroom or in the school grounds. Names for colours given by the manufacturer could be compared with those which the children suggest. Some children might go on to make up their own names for colours.

Suggestion(s) for support

Some children may require extra help with identifying the names of the colours. A set of flash cards could be produced, and children could be helped to decode the words using sound–symbol correspondence. The phonically regular nature of most names for basic colours should make this strategy particularly effective.

Assessment opportunities

Note children's abilities to identify common colours, and make particular note of those who find this difficult. It may be necessary to talk to parents about tests for colour blindness if this is suspected.

Look for signs that children are able to copy accurately and make use of their knowledge of sound–symbol correspondence to help them to spell the names of the colours.

Display ideas

Display collections of items of different colours, showing items that are shades of the same colour together. The children's completed photocopiable sheets can be put up on a wall behind the items.

Other aspects of the English PoS covered

Speaking and listening – 1c; 3a.
Reading – 2a, b.

Reference to photocopiable sheet

Photocopiable page 111 provides boxes, labelled with the names of different colours, on which the children stick appropriate pieces of coloured paper. The children then list items they have found which match the colours.

THE WASHING-LINE

To demonstrate an ability to write in sentences and to spell simple and common words.

†† *Whole class or group, working individually or in pairs.*

🕐 *One hour.*

▲ Which clothes do you think belong to each person?

Mrs Jaggs — Mr Jaggs — Andrew — Beth — baby Amy

The washing-line

Key background information
In this activity the children are provided with a picture which has a line of washing and pictures of people. They then have to write sentences which identify the owners of the clothes.

Preparation
Provide a word bank of names of clothes and of colours as a reference point for children when they are writing. Photocopy page 112, one copy for each child or pair.

Resources needed
Word bank (see above), washing-line, various items of clothing, pegs, photocopiable page 112, A4 paper, pencils, coloured pencils/crayons, felt-tipped pens. For extension activity – lost property box. For support activity – words or unfinished sentences on cards.

What to do
Introduce the activity by showing the children a washing-line in the classroom, with various items of clothing from the cloakroom pegged to it. It may be a good opportunity to identify owners of lost property or to remind children of the need to look after their clothes.

Give out copies of photocopiable page 112 and ask the children to decide which of the people own which articles of clothing. Talk with them about the clues which the pictures give as to ownership. Emphasise that there is not necessarily a right answer for each item of clothing, but that they can decide for themselves who owns what. They could begin by colouring the first item of clothing for which they are to write a sentence. Details of the colour may then be included. As they work, they should colour each item before writing about it. This will break up the writing activity.

Ask them to write sentences such as 'Mrs Jaggs owns the spotted dress'. Some may go on to elaborate and explain why they think items of clothing belong to particular people. For example, 'I think Mr Jaggs owns the large, blue shirt because he is the fattest person.'

Suggestion(s) for extension
Some children could go on to write stories about finding an item of clothing and being detectives, trying to find out to whom the clothing belongs. Alternatively, they might be given items from a lost property box and be asked to decide who has lost each item. They could make notes about each piece of clothing, suggesting what age and size the owner might be. An examination of manufacturers' labels could be encouraged to help them.

Suggestion(s) for support
Some children may require additional help with the activity in the form of cards with words written on them or pre-prepared sentences with spaces to be filled in. For example:

Mrs Jaggs owns the _____ .
Andrew wears the _____ .

Assessment opportunities
Look for evidence that children are able to write in sentences and demarcate these with capital letters and full stops. Make a note of any children who are able to expand simple sentences and look for signs that they are able to spell common words accurately.

Opportunities for IT
Pairs of children could select one article of clothing and use a word processor to write a label explaining who owns it and why they think it belongs to that person. The children

could use a large type size to make these labels, which can then be printed, cut out and attached to the clothing display.

Display ideas

A classroom washing-line could be used to display the children's coloured-in photocopiable sheets and their writing about the owners of the clothes.

Other aspects of the English PoS covered

Speaking and listening – 2a.

Reference to photocopiable sheet

Photocopiable page 112 provides a picture of a washing-line and a group of people. The children write sentences on a separate sheet to identify the owner of each item of clothing.

THE STREET

To show an ability to complete sentences.

†† *Whole class or group, working individually or in pairs.*

🕐 *One hour.*

Key background information

Much early literacy work involves matching. This activity takes matching as its starting point, but goes on to offer children opportunities to speculate. A greater understanding of the features of a sentence may be acquired through discussion of the parts of sentences provided and through talking about ways of completing or enhancing them.

Preparation

Make copies of photocopiable page 113, one for each child.

Resources needed

Photograph from a television programme, photocopiable page 113, writing pencils, coloured pencils, chalkboard, coloured chalk, word bank of colours. Word cards for support activity.

What to do

It might be a good idea to introduce this activity by showing the children a picture of a familiar street from a television programme. This could be Ramsay Street from *Neighbours*, *Coronation Street*, or the main street in Greendale from *Postman Pat*.

On the board draw a simple picture of a row of houses and simple pictures of people (these

could be matchstick figures) with names written underneath. Ask the children to take turns to colour one of the doors and to decide which of the people live in which house. Write sentences to show who lives where on the board.

When the children seem familiar with the activity, give out the photocopiable sheets and explain that they should colour the houses and then complete the sentences by looking at the names of the people and writing in the spaces the name of each person and the colour of each house. If children are not already familiar with the spellings of common colours provide a word bank of these.

Suggestion(s) for extension

The children could draw their own streets and decide on names for people who live in the different houses and then write sentences. They could write about the characteristics of different people and could invent families and jobs for them. Some may go on to write stories about the characters in their streets.

Suggestion(s) for support

Children who find the activity difficult could work with partners or with an adult. Cards could be prepared with the names of the people, the colours and the words 'house' 'lives' and 'in the'. Children could then physically manipulate the text and write sentences copying from the cards.

Assessment opportunities

Note the children's abilities to copy names accurately and to use capital letters appropriately. Look for evidence that they are able to complete sentences.

Opportunities for IT

The children could use a word processor to write about the people who live in one of the houses on the photocopiable sheet, or the houses they have drawn. These could be printed out and used as part of the class display.

Display ideas

A large picture of a street could be produced, with each child drawing or painting a house, each one being mounted on the frieze. Sentences could be written next to pictures of people, and children might be invited to read these and decide where different people live.

Other aspects of the English PoS covered

Speaking and listening – 1c.
Reading – 2b.

Reference to photocopiable sheet

Photocopiable page 113 provides a picture of a row of houses and pictures of people who live in them. The names of the people are written below each person and the children fill in the accompanying sentences.

use capital letters to begin them and to use full stops at the end.

Preparation

Prepare a list of names of domestic animals as an aid to spelling. It would be a good idea to add pictures of each animal to help with reading. Make copies of photocopiable page 114, one for each child. Collect photographs of people and pets for the extension activity.

Resources needed

List of animals (each one with a picture, if possible), photocopiable page 114, writing materials. Photographs of people and pets for extension activity. Cards with key words/ phrases for support activity.

PETS AND OWNERS

To be able to write in sentences and to use capital letters and full stops appropriately.

†† *Whole class or group, working individually or in pairs.*
⏰ *One hour.*

Key background information

It has been said that pet owners often resemble their pets! In this activity children are presented with a photocopiable sheet which has pictures of people and pictures of pets. They have to join the people to the pets by drawing a line. They then choose names for the pets and write them underneath the pictures of the pets. They can go on to write sentences such as 'Emma Hampton has a pet dog called Suzy'. As children develop their abilities to write in sentences it is important to draw their attention to the need to

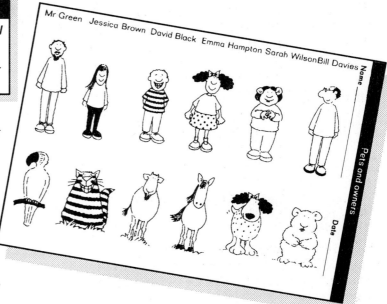

What to do

Tell the children that some people say that pets and owners sometimes look alike. Talk about the pets which the children have and ask them about the pets they would like to have.

Show the children the photocopiable sheet and ask them to look at the pictures of the pets and the people on their copies. Ask them to think about which person might own which pet. Tell them that there is no right answer, but that you have done the exercise and you wonder if your ideas are the same as theirs. Then ask the children to draw a line to link a person to a pet and to write a name for each pet. On a separate piece of paper they should write a sentence which uses the name of the person and the pet. Encourage the use of adjectives to enhance the sentences by providing descriptions of the pets and the owners.

Suggestion(s) for extension

Some children could look at pictures of pets and decide what the owners would be like and draw pictures and write descriptions of them. Alternatively, children could be provided with photographs of people and be asked to write about suitable pets for them.

Suggestion(s) for support

Some children may need to dictate their sentences to a writing partner. They could go on to copy the sentences. Alternatively, they could be given cards with key words and phrases to enable them to build up sentences. These might include:

I think   belongs to

has a pet   owns

It is important that the phrases are read with the children so that they know what the words say.

Assessment opportunities

Note the children's abilities to use capital letters appropriately and to write in complete sentences. Look, also, at their abilities to copy spellings accurately where these have been provided.

Display ideas

A display of pictures of the pets which belong to members of the class could be put up as a stimulus to further work on this topic. Children could be asked to identify the owners and write reasons for their decisions.

Other aspects of the English PoS covered

Reading – 2b.

Reference to photocopiable sheet

Photocopiable page 114 provides pictures of pets and owners for children to match, as a prelude to writing sentences. The children write names for the pets under the pictures.

PACKAGING A PRODUCT

To demonstrate developing letter formation skills and clear and neat presentation.

†† *Whole class or group, working individually or in pairs.*

🕐 *One hour.*

Key background information

This activity is designed to develop presentational skills by asking the children to design their own box or label for a well-known product. This activity could be linked to the activities based on shopping on pages 90 to 92.

Preparation

Bring to school a selection of packages for products. Look in particular for those which have large writing and which might be familiar to the children.

Resources needed

Examples of packages (see above), writing and drawing materials.

What to do

Show the children some of the packages and talk with them about the ways in which some words are printed very large, while others are smaller. Ask the children why they think this is, and discuss the ways in which the packaging might persuade them to buy the product.

Ask the children to think about a product which they like or one which they think could be presented better. Tell them that they are going to design their own packaging and explain that they will need to include the name of the product and some other details, such as ingredients for food, and that they may add other words to make the product look more interesting to prospective buyers.

Encourage the children to try to be original in their ideas and not simply to copy the existing packaging.

Suggestion(s) for extension

Examples of the children's work could be copied and sent to manufacturers, together with letters from the children. It may be advisable to write to manufacturers in advance. Letters should usually be addressed to the public relations officer. Some children may wish to invent a product and create packaging for it.

Suggestion(s) for support

Some children may need to work with an adult to develop letter formation and copying skills. It may be necessary for you to write words faintly in pencil for the child to trace over with pencil and then with felt-tipped pen.

Assessment opportunities

Look for signs that children are forming letters correctly and are able to present their work clearly and neatly.

Opportunities for IT

Children could use a word processor or simple art package to write a label for their packaging, giving some details about the product. They could select different fonts and change the colour or size.

Display ideas

The packages could be included in the class shop in place of the commercially produced originals.

Other aspects of the English PoS covered

Speaking and listening – 1a, b, c.
Reading – 1c; 2b.

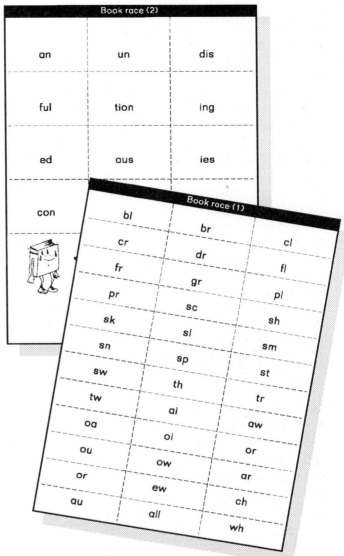

BOOK RACE

To demonstrate increasing knowledge of sound–symbol correspondence and phonological patterns.
†† *Whole class or group, working in small groups or in pairs.*
⏲ *One hour.*

Previous skills/knowledge needed

Children will need to be acquainted with common sound–symbol relationships and should be ready to move on to a closer examination of digraphs and blends.

Key background information

In this activity children take turns to take a card from a pile, on the reverse of which is a blend or digraph which are common beginnings for English words. (A blend is made when two or more letters come together but retain their individual sounds, as in 'bl', 'cr', 'sl' and 'st'. A digraph is a single sound such as 'ch', 'sh' or 'ou' made by combining two letters.) The children then have to look through their reading books and write down all the words which they can find that begin with the letters on the card.

Preparation

Make copies of photocopiable pages 115 and 116 on to card or photocopy the sheets on to paper and then paste on card. Laminate if possible and then cut out the cards. Alternatively, cut out the cards from copies of the photocopiable sheets and paste on to old playing cards. On the board write a passage which the children will be able to read quite easily.

Resources needed

The children's reading books, photocopiable page 115, chalkboard, writing materials. Photocopiable page 116 for extension activity.

What to do

Show the children one of the sound cards and ask them to see if they can find an example of a word in the passage that you have written on the board which has that sound at the beginning or somewhere within it. When they do, either write the word on the board or let the children take turns to write the words on the board.

When the children are familiar with the activity, provide them with the sound cards made from photocopiable page 115 and ask them to use their reading books to find as many examples as they can of words with each sound and then to write these down. Tell the children that you want them to be very careful with spelling, so they will need to look at the words which they copy in some detail.

Stop the children regularly to check that they are able not only to recognise graphemes, but also to describe the sound that they make. Discuss the sound–symbol relationships with the whole class or group, and show them examples of what each pair or group has found.

Suggestion(s) for extension
Some children could go on to use the second photocopiable sheet which includes more complex letter strings, prefixes and suffixes. They might use more advanced reading materials too.

Suggestion(s) for support
Those children who struggle with blends and digraphs might begin by using single letters and a limited number of initial blends and digraphs such as 'st', 'br', 'bl' and 'sh', 'th' and 'wh'.

Assessment opportunities
The activity should allow you to assess children's phonic awareness and their abilities to relate the sounds which they read to those which they write.

Display ideas
Display a piece of writing. This may be copied from a book with which the children are familiar. On separate pieces of card or paper write some examples of graphemes. Use wool or string to link these to words within the text. The children could use the display to find further examples and to look for other graphemes which they learn subsequently.

Other aspects of the English PoS covered
Reading – 2b.

Reference to photocopiable sheets
Photocopiable page 115 provides graphemes which are common beginnings for English words. Photocopiable page 116 gives examples of longer letter strings. Both sheets are used to make cards for the 'Book race' activity.

WHERE WOULD YOU FIND IT?

To produce writing based upon close reading of words which are found in the classroom.
†† *Whole class, working in small groups.*
🕐 *One hour.*

Key background information
This activity is designed both to develop children's knowledge of the geography of their own classroom and to develop writing of the names of equipment used in the classroom. The labelling of cupboards and drawers is an important feature of primary classrooms. It serves not only to develop children's purposeful reading but also enables teachers to develop pupils' independence by providing signs which allow them to find things for themselves.

Preparation
Ensure that cupboards and drawers to which children have access are clearly labelled. Make a selection of items which children use regularly.

Resources needed
Various items taken from cupboards and drawers in the classroom, writing materials, chalkboard. Word bank for support activity.

What to do
Show the children a series of items which are kept in various parts of the classroom. Ask them to tell you whereabouts the items would be kept and write the names of the places such as 'cupboard', 'shelf' and 'drawer' on the board. Ask the children in turn to take the items and put them away in the right places and encourage them to read the labels in the various places in the classroom.

With the children working in groups, provide each group with a selection of items and ask them to write the names of the items and the places where they belong in sentences. An example should be provided, such as 'The scissors live in the yellow drawer.' Labels on drawers and cupboards could then be designed and illustrated by the children.

Suggestion(s) for extension
Children could write about ways in which classroom organisation might be improved. They could draw plans and

describe where they think different items could be stored so that they were easily accessible. For example, they might consider which items were used most frequently and decide to position them in the most accessible place.

Suggestion(s) for support
The activity might be undertaken by children using *Breakthrough to Literacy* materials (David Mackay *et al.*, Longman) suitably extended. A word bank of useful words should be provided to help all children with spellings.

Assessment opportunities
Note the children's abilities to look carefully at words and write them accurately. Note examples of letter reversal and transposition of letters.

Opportunities for IT
The children could use a concept keyboard linked to a word processor to write sentences about where different things live. Alternatively, you could prepare and save a word processed file which gives the beginning of the sentences for example 'The crayons live in ...' and allow the children to type in the missing words. The activity will provide opportunities to load the file and use the mouse or cursor keys to move around the list of sentences.

paintbrushes

Display ideas
Children's plans for a well-organised classroom could be displayed, together with their writing. The labels made by the children will improve the appearance of all parts of the classroom.

Other aspects of the English PoS covered
Reading – 1b.

PEOPLE WHO HELP US

To produce simple writing and sentence writing.
†† *Whole class or group, working individually or in pairs.*
🕐 *One hour.*

Key background information
In this activity children draw and write the names of people who help them. They will be involved in looking at the names of helpers and in writing these. Some may go on to write sentences. The activity may be attempted at a very simple level with the emphasis upon copying skills, or may be undertaken at a more advanced level with independent work from the children.

Preparation
Create a word bank of names of people who help us. This might include the following:

teacher	parent
doctor	nurse
policeman	policewoman
fire-fighter	lifeguard
crossing patrol	dinner supervisor

Resources needed
Word bank, writing and drawing materials. Reference books which include information on jobs for extension activity. Word cards for support activity.

What to do
Ask the children to think about the people who help them every day. If they find this difficult at first, mention parents, crossing patrols, dinner supervisors and so on. Talk through a typical school day and list all the people who help during the day.

Ask the children to draw pictures of helpful people and label them. Some may find this sufficiently challenging. Many may be able to go on to write sentences such as 'The lollipop man helps us to cross the road' or 'The doctor helps us because she makes us better when we are ill.'

Offer the children a structure for their sentences so that they might begin with the job title, then write 'helps us' and then write what it is that the person helps us to do. Some children may move on from this to create their own sentence structures, but others may require the security of a simple format.

Show the children examples of sentences written by those who are working well, and use these as examples for those who are finding the activity more difficult.

Suggestion(s) for extension
Children could find out more about the jobs done by people who help us, and could use books to find information which would help them to write at greater length.

Suggestion(s) for support

Appropriate words could be written on card for children to use to supplement their own vocabularies. Alternatively, *Breakthrough* materials could be added to.

Assessment opportunities

During the activity look for evidence that children are able to copy words accurately and, in some cases, are able to write complete sentences.

Opportunities for IT

Children could use an art or drawing package to draw a picture of one of the people who helps them. The picture could be added to the sentence about that person written on a word processor. Children can experiment with different-size fonts and positioning the picture in different places on the page. The pages can be printed out and bound as a class book.

It may be possible to set up a simple multimedia presentation using authoring software where a list of helpful people appears on the title screen, and the children's own pictures and writing are linked to the list, so that clicking on the policeman displays the appropriate picture and writing.

Display ideas

Large pictures of helpful people could be displayed on the wall, together with the children's writing. An alternative, if possible, could be to dress a tailor's dummy in the uniform of a helpful person and to display the writing next to it.

Other aspects of the English PoS covered

Speaking and listening – 1a.

QUESTIONS

To be able to use question marks and to write sentences.

†† *Whole class, working in pairs or small groups.*

🕒 *One hour, and 40 minutes the next day.*

Key background information

Many of the sentences which children use when speaking take the form of questions. This activity is designed to develop children's abilities to use question marks. They are asked to make up questions about a topic which they are about to study. The questions are handed in to you, and then you can use them as part of your introduction to the topic. This activity could be introduced by playing a tape recording of children speaking and then asking pupils to identify the questions they heard.

Preparation

Prepare a list of key words related to the topic or subject area which the children are about to study, and display prominently. If possible, make a tape recording of children's conversations.

Resources needed

Topic word list, writing materials, chalkboard, reference books. Cassette player and tape recording of children's conversations (optional).

What to do

If you have a tape recording of children's conversations, play this to the children and ask them to listen carefully to identify when questions were asked. Talk with them about the questions and write some of them on the board. Discuss the use of question marks and ask the children to tell you where to put them.

Tell the children a little about the topic they are going to study. Explain that you would like them to think about the topic and also about the things which they would like to know about it. Ask them to think of some questions which they would like answered, so that you can either answer them or help the children to do so.

Ask them to work in pairs or small groups to devise questions, writing them down so that they will be able to pass them on to you. Tell each group that they should produce at least three questions. When they have done this, ask them to look at their questions and check that they have included capital letters and question marks.

Gather together the class, each group with their questions, and ask the children to read some of the questions aloud. Tell the children that you will look at the questions and try to answer some of them tomorrow. Explain that you will need to look up some of the answers and that you will need to use reference books to do this. Explain that some of the questions will be answered later as the topic develops.

The following day, tell the children that you are going to answer at least one of each group's questions and, as you do, talk about how you found the answers. Draw the children's attention to the reference books for the topic and explain that they, too, could use these to answer questions.

Reiterate the importance of using question marks to make clear to the reader that questions are sentences which require an answer rather than just statements.

Suggestion(s) for extension
Some children could go on to formulate questions for each other. Reference books could be used to pose the questions, and to answer them.

Suggestion(s) for support
Children who might experience difficulty in formulating questions could be placed in groups with those who are more able.

Assessment opportunities
Look for evidence of appropriate use of capital letters and question marks and note children's abilities to organise their sentences accurately.

Opportunities for IT
Each of the groups could type out one or all of their questions for a class list or display. The children should be shown how to add question marks using the appropriate key with the shift key.

Display ideas
A question and answers board could be created, with questions connected with the topic being written on the board by the children and by you. This will encourage research using information books.

Other aspects of the English PoS covered
Speaking and listening – 1a.
Reading – 2d.

CAPITAL LETTERS

To use capital letters accurately and to be able to explain their usage.

†† *Whole class or group, working individually or in pairs.*
🕐 *At least one hour.*

Previous skills/knowledge needed
The children will need to be familiar with the terms capital letter and full stop.

Key background information
In this activity the children will learn that capital letters are used at the beginnings of sentences, for the first word in a line of poetry and for direct quotations. They are also used for the important words in titles of books, songs and so on. Some words always use a capital letter no matter where they appear in a sentence: for example, the word 'I'; for initials; for the titles of people such as Mr, Mrs, Ms and Dr; and for the names of people, places, days and months.

This activity is intended to develop children's knowledge of the use of capital letters and to provide you with an opportunity to assess their understanding.

[worksheet: Capital letters (1)]

Name _____ Date _____

▲ Look at the words on this sheet. Some of them should begin with capital letters. Find the words which need capital letters and write them correctly in the space under each word. Then write why the word needs a capital letter. The first word has been done for you.

london	scotland	city	wales
London	place		
whales	i	me	man
mountain	ben nevis	france	country
friday	april	month	james

Preparation
Copy photocopiable pages 117 and 118 (you will need both sheets for each child or pair) and find examples of titles, names, places and so on which have initial capital letters.

Resources needed
Examples of the use of capital letters taken from books, magazines and newspapers, photocopiable pages 117 and 118, chalkboard, writing materials.

What to do

Show the children the examples of the use of capital letters which you have found and ask them if they can tell you why some letters are written differently from others. Talk, in particular, about names and show the children how their names are written with capitals at the beginning of each word.

On the board, write a list of some of the kinds of words which need capital letters, for example:
▲ names of people;
▲ names of places;
▲ months;
▲ days of the week;
▲ streets;
▲ I;
▲ God, or the name for God such as Allah;
▲ titles.

Show the children photocopiable page 117 and talk with them about some of the words. Ask them to suggest which ones should have capital letters. When they seem confident about this, ask them to look at the sheet individually or in pairs and write those words which need capital letters correctly in the spaces provided. In the second space provided for each word they should write the reason for the capital letter. They only need to write 'place', 'name' and so on.

When the children have completed the sheet and have shown that they understand the use of capital letters, give them a copy of photocopiable page 118 and ask them to look at the piece of writing and to circle in pencil those words which they think should be capitalised. Then the children can finish the Goldilocks story, using capital letters correctly.

To conclude the activity, an oral session could be held in which you read a passage from a book and the children put up their hands every time they hear a word which they think begins with a capital letter.

Suggestion(s) for extension

Children could be asked to make a collection of titles, headlines, names etc. which are printed in lower case and have initial capital letters. They could then make a display with brief explanations for the inclusion of each capital letter written next to the examples.

Suggestion(s) for support

Those children whose reading abilities are limited should be provided with simple one-syllable words to work on. Although

---

Capital letters (2)

Name _____ Date _____

▲ This story has no capital letters. Read it carefully and then circle the words which you think should begin with a capital letter.

once upon a time there were three bears. there was a daddy bear, mummy bear and baby bear and they all lived together in a little house in the woods.

one day, just after daddy bear had made some porridge for breakfast, mummy bear said, 'let's go out for a little walk until the porridge has cooled', so they all set off into the woods.

while they were gone a little girl, called goldilocks, crept into their house and began to look around. she saw three bowls of porridge and tried each one before eating all of baby bear's.

goldilocks felt tired after eating so much porridge, so she decided to sit down. she tried two big chairs, but she did not like them. then she tried a little chair which belonged to baby bear, but when she sat on it the chair broke and she fell on to the floor.

goldilocks felt very sore after her fall, but she still climbed the stairs to the bears' bedroom. there were three beds and she tried lying on each one. she decided that she liked the small one best and she lay down and put her head on the pillow. very soon goldilocks fell asleep.

▲ How does the story end? Can you write the ending? Make sure you use capital letters in the right places.

---

the activity may help to develop vocabularies, this is not the main objective. The use of easy-to-read words should enable the children to concentrate on the concept of capital letters without encountering reading difficulties.

Assessment opportunities

Look for evidence that children are able to identify consistently those words which require capital letters and note their abilities to explain the reasons for their use.

Display ideas

A display of examples of capital letter usage found by the children attempting the extension activity could provide a point of reference for the class. A page of a story which is familiar to the children could be enlarged and be displayed for the children to look at. Each capital letter could be highlighted and the children could be asked to look at the display and discuss the reasons for the use of the capital letters.

Other aspects of the English PoS covered

Reading – 2b; 3.

Reference to photocopiable sheets

Photocopiable page 117 provides a list of words, some of which require capital letters. Photocopiable page 118 comprises a passage with no capital letters which the children read and then try to identify those words which require capitals.

MAKING SENTENCES

To demonstrate understanding of the ways in which phrases and clauses can link together to make sentences.

†† *Whole class or group, working individually or in pairs.*

⏱ *One hour.*

Previous skills/knowledge needed

Children attempting this activity will need to have reading abilities which enable them to read the parts of sentences provided on photocopiable page 119. They will also need to be aware that sentences begin with capital letters and end with full stops, question marks or exclamation marks. A simple definition of a sentence, such as, 'A sentence says something about a person or a thing', should be discussed with the children.

Key background information

The sentence is a grammatical construction which can stand alone, without the reader feeling that it is incomplete. Although sentences may be grouped together to form larger units such as paragraphs, individual sentences may still convey meaning without the context which larger units of text provide.

This activity requires children to combine phrases and clauses to make complete sentences. It is not necessary to use the terms 'phrase' and 'clause' at this stage, but some children may be introduced to them. However, the definitions which describe the distinction between the two may prove problematical. A phrase cannot stand alone as it does not have a verb, while a clause includes a verb and its subject and may make a complete sentence by itself.

Preparation

Make up some short sentences and decide upon suitable places where they could be divided. Write these on strips of card and cut each one into two parts. Make copies of photocopiable page 119, one for each child or pair. Photocopy page 120 for children doing the extension activity.

Resources needed

Strips of card, photocopiable pages 119 and 120, chalkboard, Blu-Tack, writing materials.

What to do

Mount the phrases and clauses separately from each other on the board and read through them with the children. Now ask the children to suggest which parts of the sentences could be combined to make complete sentences. Draw their attention to the capital letters and full stops, and make sure that they know that the parts with capital letters will be the first parts of the sentences and those with full stops will be the final parts. The parts of the sentences may be moved by the children and the completed sentences read aloud to see if they make sense.

When the children seem confident about manipulating text in this way, give out copies of photocopiable page 119 and explain that the sheet has parts of sentences which can be combined to make full sentences. At first the children can simply draw lines linking the parts together, but, once they have shown that they can combine the sentences effectively, they can go on to write their sentences on paper.

Discuss the children's sentences with them and bring the class or group together to talk about the solutions which they found. Reinforce the concept of sentences by writing more examples on the board, this time just using initial phrases and clauses and asking the children to make up final ones. Follow this by providing final phrases and clauses only and asking the children to make up initial ones.

Suggestion(s) for extension

Photocopiable page 120 provides phrases and clauses which may be used to make up a variety of sentences. This time the children may use each phrase or clause as many times as they like to create lots of combinations for their sentences. The objective is for them to develop their understanding of the possible ways in which sentences may be constructed.

For those children who require further extension work, a

Making sentences (2)

Name _____ Date _____

▲ Use the parts of sentences as many times as you like to make as many sentences as you can. Write your sentences on paper.

The big, black car	was good at dancing.
A white horse	drove up the hill.
A ginger cat	did not like carrots.
Rebecca Smart	loved to eat carrots.
Simon and Peter	stood a silver fairy.
The young girl	it was dark and cold.
On top of the tree	liked reading books.
Inside the cave	hid under the chair.
A little mouse	keeps you warm.
A woollen h...	...imal

Making sentences (1)

Name _____ Date _____

▲ Can you join the parts of sentences to make complete sentences? One has been done for you.

The snowball	a bone in its mouth.
The dog had	high in the sky.
The aeroplane flew	in my pocket.
I found 20 pence	was cold and wet.
Sita could not find	and started to cry.
Luke kicked the ball	her favourite doll.
Adam sat on the floor	through the window.
Heather and Sophie	were best friends.
It was a hot day	when the lion roared.
Everyone was afraid	and the sun shone.

set of subordinate clauses such as 'who had red hair' and 'who wore a blue coat' might be provided for them to add to their sentences.

Suggestion(s) for support

Children who find the activity difficult should be allowed to cut out the sentences from photocopiable page 119 and physically move the text around to try different combinations, which may be read to a partner before being written down.

Assessment opportunities

Look for evidence that children understand the concept of a sentence. Note their abilities to recognise the initial and final parts of the sentence by looking at the capital letters and full stops. Look for evidence that they are able to create grammatically feasible combinations of initial and final phrases and clauses.

Display ideas

Label a display board with the title 'Making sentences'. Write on card separate phrases and clauses which can be combined to make sentences and include those which you used to initiate the activity. Make sure that the display is at a height which children can reach, and create a display which the children can use to try out different sentence combinations by moving the cards around.

Other aspects of the English PoS covered

Speaking and listening – 2b; 3a.
Reading – 2a, b.

Reference to photocopiable sheets

Photocopiable page 119 provides phrases and clauses which children can combine to make complete sentences. Photocopiable page 120, which is to be used for the extension activity, provides a larger number of phrases and clauses which may be combined to make as many sentences as the children are capable of creating.

COMMAS

To demonstrate a developing understanding of the use of commas to separate words in lists.

†† *Whole class or group, working individually or in pairs.*
🕐 *Up to one hour.*

Previous skills/knowledge needed

Children attempting this activity need to have been aware of commas in their reading and should understand the basic concept of the sentence and the use of full stops.

Key background information

The most basic function of the comma is to separate parts of a sentence. In this activity the focus is upon the use of commas in lists. Listing is one of the most common features of young children's writing and, as lists begin to find their way into sentences, children should be introduced to the idea of using commas to separate items. Commas should be placed in between each item, but they are not usually required where a conjunction such as 'and' is used.

Preparation

Write some sentences on the board which include lists. These might include:

For my birthday I was given a doll, a jigsaw, a book about ballet and a football.
I have four sisters who are called Jenna, Nicole, Rachel and Debbie.
In the zoo there are lions, tigers, elephants, monkeys and camels.

Make copies of photocopiable page 121, one for each child or pair.

Resources needed

Photocopiable page 121, chalkboard, writing materials.

What to do

Show the children the sentences which you have written on the board. Show them what a comma looks like and ask them to find the commas in the sentences. Ask the children if they can suggest any reasons why the commas are placed where they are. Either tell them or elicit from them that the commas separate the items in a list.

Next, write some sentences which include lists, but which do not have commas. For example:

My sister is clever pretty happy and popular.
Paul had dark hair blue eyes and lots of freckles.
London is big busy noisy and full of things to do.

Ask the children to read the sentences aloud and to think about where commas should be placed to separate the items in the lists. When you are satisfied that the children have understood the concept of using commas in lists, give out copies of photocopiable page 121. The first section simply

Language study

requires the children to write commas in pencil in the appropriate places. The final section has pictures of people with adjectives written beneath their names. On a separate sheet of paper the children have to use the names and the adjectives to create sentences which include commas.

As the children work, stop them occasionally to discuss progress and to reinforce the concept by working through examples on the board.

Suggestion(s) for extension

Ask those children whom you feel are able to do so, to think of and then write sentences of their own which include commas being used in lists. Some children could also look through books to find further examples and a discussion of other uses of commas might be held during group reading sessions.

Suggestion(s) for support

In order to help children who are unsure about the placement of commas it may be a good idea to read the sentences on the photocopiable sheet aloud and make slightly exaggerated pauses at the places where commas should be placed. Ask the children to raise their hands or say 'comma' when they think one should appear.

Assessment opportunities

Note the children's abilities to apply the knowledge which they have gained when they write sentences of their own. Listen for evidence that they appreciate the comma's function when they are reading aloud.

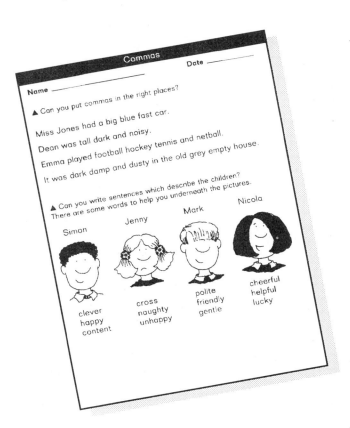

Opportunities for IT

The children could take it in turns to use a word processor and make up lists of their own, using the commas in the correct places. They should be shown where the comma key is located, making sure that they do not confuse it with the apostrophe key.

Display ideas

A display of sentences which include lists could be presented on a display board which is at an appropriate height for the children to reach. Small pieces of card with commas drawn upon them could be placed in a box and the children could be asked to pin them in the right places in the sentences. The display could also include some of the sentences which children create themselves in the extension activity.

Other aspects of the English PoS covered

Reading – 2a, b.

Reference to photocopiable sheet

Photocopiable page 121 provides sentences which include lists and require commas, and sets of names and characteristics which the children can put into sentences.

UN- AND -ING RACE

To demonstrate an increased knowledge of common prefixes and suffixes.

†† *Whole class or group.*

🕐 *1 hour initially, but the activity may continue with children making individual or group collections of words.*

Previous skills/knowledge needed

Children will need to have some awareness of sound–symbol correspondence and should be able to break words up into their constituent parts.

Key background information

Some beginnings and endings of words in English are very common and usually follow the same rules each time they are used. A prefix is a syllable or syllables affixed to the front of a word in order to alter its meaning in a predictable way. The prefix 'un-', for instance, changes a word into its opposite. A suffix is a syllable added to the end of a word to change its grammatical function. The suffix '-ing' changes the aspect of a verb into the present participle, describing the action of the verb as an ongoing situation, for example, pick becomes picking – 'In the summer we pick apples from the tree'. 'The sun shone on us picking apples from the tree'.

Resources needed

Simple dictionaries, chalkboard, display chart, writing materials. Word bank for support activity.

What to do

Discuss, at a simple level, prefixes and suffixes and the ways in which they are used. Ask the children to think of some words which they could prefix with 'un-'. Write some contributions on the board. If they find this difficult, talk about opposites, using examples such as 'happy' and 'unhappy', 'tidy' and 'untidy'. Suggest some words to them and ask them to use 'un-' to make an opposite meaning.

Repeat the exercise with '-ing'. You could use actions to encourage the children to think about when we use this part of the verb. For example, you could say to them 'I write with chalk' and then pick up the chalk and as you write say, 'I am writing with chalk.' Let them take turns to use verbs in the same way. Ask them to work in small groups to produce as many '-ing' and 'un-' words as possible within a short period of time. One child in each group could act as a scribe. Bring the class together and record some of each group's words on a chart which will be displayed on the wall. Set the children a challenge to add as many words as possible to each list over a week. Some could concentrate on '-ing' words and others on 'un-' words. They could add words during reading sessions or at the ends of lessons. Encourage the use of simple dictionaries and tell the children that they are allowed to get ideas from adults or others at home.

Suggestion(s) for extension

Make collections of other prefixes and suffixes such as 'dis-' and '-ed'. Talk with the children about what happens when a word which ends in 'e' has '-ing' added to it. Discuss the doubling of consonants when '-ed' or '-ing' are added to words.

The children could arrange the 'un-' and '-ing' words in alphabetical order. Alternatively, you could ask the children to write a story which includes a set number of '-ing' or 'un-' words.

Suggestion(s) for support

Have a bank of simple examples of each category for children to sort and then add to their team's record. These might include words such as 'going', 'coming', 'saying', 'using', 'unusual', 'unhelpful', 'undone' and 'unfriendly'.

Assessment opportunities

Monitor each child's contributions to assess whether prefixes and suffixes have been understood.

Opportunities for IT

Children could use a word processor to type and print their own additions to a class display of words. These should be printed out in a font large enough to be read from a distance.

Other aspects of the English PoS covered

Reading – 2b.

NO MORE MR NICE GUY

To use imaginative vocabulary choices and to demonstrate an awareness of adjectives and their function.

†† *Group of children who are about to produce a piece of writing, followed by individual work.*

🕐 *One hour for initial activity. 30 minutes for follow-up.*

Key background information
In this activity children are asked to replace the word 'nice' with more interesting adjectives in a series of sentences. The activity is intended to draw children's attention to the range of possible adjectives which might be used to make their writing more interesting. Teachers often criticise the use of the word 'nice' because it does not allow precision in description. However, children should not be forbidden to use it. Rather, they should be encouraged to think of alternatives.

Preparation
Make copies of photocopiable page 122, one copy for each child. Prepare a list of alternative words to the word 'nice' for the support activity.

Resources needed
Photocopiable page 122, chalkboard (or large piece of paper), writing materials. Children's thesaurus and reading books for extension activity. A list of adjectives for the support activity.

What to do
Begin the activity by reading the passage from photocopiable page 122 to the children and asking them about it. The repetition of the word 'nice' should be noticed, but, if it is not, draw children's attention to it. Ask them if there are other words which could be used instead of 'nice' in different situations.

Draw a circle in the middle of the board and write the word 'nice' in it. Ask the children for their suggestions for alternatives and write these around the circle with lines radiating from it to the words.

When the children have discussed the words ask them to work through the passage on the photocopiable sheet and replace the word 'nice' wherever possible, writing their replacement words above the word 'nice'. Encourage them to use a variety of different words. It is important that children understand that there is no correct replacement for the word 'nice' and that they may choose any appropriate words. Stop them periodically to discuss the words which they have used and to write some of them on the board to help with spellings and to provide ideas for others.

Completed pieces of work could be read aloud by the children and discussed with the class or group.

A nice day

Name _____ Date _____

In the summer I had a really nice time when we went to the seaside. The sky was blue and it was a really nice day. After a nice easy drive we reached Bridlington at 10 o'clock in the morning.

When we had parked the car in a nice street we walked to the beach. The sand was nice and clean, and the sea was a nice deep blue colour. We made sandcastles and Mum bought us some nice flags to stick into them. My sister had a nice time burying my dad in the sand until only his head could be seen. I can't wait to see the photographs!

On the way home we stopped at a café and had some really nice cakes and a nice cold drink and Mum and Dad had a nice cup of tea.

Suggestion(s) for extension
Some children could use a simple thesaurus to help them to find alternatives. The children might also be asked to look at simple reading books and to suggest additional adjectives or alternatives to some of those which are used.

The activity should provide a starting point for children to think about vocabulary use when producing an independent piece of writing.

Suggestion(s) for support
Children who experience difficulties could be provided with a list of adjectives from which they could choose words to complete the exercise.

Assessment opportunities
Note children's abilities to make imaginative vocabulary choices and to read their work aloud and discuss their use of adjectives.

Opportunities for IT
Some children could use a word processor to edit a prepared file of the passage. They could use the mouse or cursor keys to move around the text, replacing the word 'nice' with ones from the class list. They could then highlight the new word in italics or bold and print out the list for class display. More able children could even use the search and replace command to locate all the instances of the word 'nice'!

Display ideas

A 'nice' chart, on the lines of the one produced at the beginning of the lesson or in the 'Opportunities for IT', could be put on the wall as a visual aid for future writing and children could be encouraged to refer to it and add to it over a period of time.

Other aspects of the English PoS covered

Speaking and listening – 3b.
Reading – 1a.

Reference to photocopiable sheet

Photocopiable page 122 provides a passage in which the word 'nice' is used extensively. Children should try to replace the word wherever possible with alternative adjectives.

CODED MESSAGES

To demonstrate an increased understanding of the importance of correct word order in sentences.

†† *Whole class or group, working individually.*

🕐 *About one hour.*

Key background information

In this activity children are presented with jumbled sentences which they restructure to make logical sentences. Word order has an important effect on the meaning conveyed by a sentence. For example:

The dog bit the man.
The man bit the dog.
I get what I like.
I like what I get.
Say what you mean.
Mean what you say.

The activity should enable children to see that the order in which words are presented is crucial to clarity of meaning.

Preparation

Write some jumbled sentences on the board. Make copies of photocopiable page 123, one for each child. Prepare shorter sentences for children needing support work, as well as words on separate pieces of card which can make sentences when placed in sequence.

Resources needed

Examples of jumbled sentences on a chalkboard or large sheet of paper, photocopiable page 123, writing materials. Word cards for support activity (see 'Preparation').

Coded messages

Name _____ Date _____

▲ Can you put the words in the right order and then answer the questions?

name is What your?

old you How are?

name teacher What the is of your?

day today What is it?

brothers Do have you sisters and any?

name school your What the is of?

try Now to write sentences jumbled your own of.

What to do

Show the children the jumbled sentences on the board and ask them if they can work out the right order for the words. The first word in the correct sentence should have a capital letter so that children have an idea of where to start.

When you have worked through the examples ask the children if they can think of a jumbled sentence of their own. Let them try this on paper and remind them that they must use all of the words in the sentence when they jumble it up. Tell them, too, that the first word of the correct sentence should have a capital letter and that there should be a full stop or a question mark at the end.

When the children are ready to

do so ask them to look at the photocopiable sheet and let them try to unscramble the sentences, write them correctly and then write a reply.

Children could go on to send jumbled messages to friends and a written coded dialogue could take place.

Suggestion(s) for extension
Those children who are capable of doing so could go on to write longer and more complex jumbled sentences.

Suggestion(s) for support
Children who find the activity difficult could be given very short sentences or words written on cards so that they can physically manipulate the words.

Assessment opportunities
Note the children's understanding of the importance of word order in providing clarity of meaning.

Opportunities for IT
You could set up a number of jumbled messages using a drawing package, where each word in the sentence is typed in separately so that they can be picked up and moved around the screen and placed in the correct order. A similar activity could be achieved using framework software like *My World 2*.

Older or more able children may be able to do the same activity using a word processor with a 'drag and drop' facility so that words can easily be moved around the screen.

Display ideas
Children could write enlarged versions of their messages which could be displayed for others to decode.

Other aspects of the English PoS covered
Reading – 2a.

Reference to photocopiable sheet
Photocopiable page 123 provides jumbled sentences which the children should restructure and respond to.

MAKING A COLLECTION OF WRITING

To demonstrate increased awareness of the features of different types of writing.
†† *Group, working individually.*
🕐 *Open-ended initially then one hour.*

Key background information
In this activity children make a collection of different pieces of writing such as parents' shopping lists, letters (with parents' permission), stories, poems and so on. They then write a description of their collections for display alongside the collections. The activity is intended not only to develop the children's writing skills but also to foster an awareness of the range and scope of writing.

Preparation
Ask the children to make a collection of writing at home and in school. A letter to parents may encourage their co-operation. Tell them that they can bring examples from newspapers, magazines, letters, lists – in fact any pieces of writing which they can find and which their parents are happy for them to bring to school.

Resources needed
Examples of writing (see above), sugar paper, writing materials.

What to do
Talk with the children about the collections of writing which they have brought to school and which they have collected in the classroom. Discuss the different kinds of print and handwriting and ask the children to tell you about the purpose of each piece.

Ask the children about presentation of writing and discuss when it is important that writing is very neat and when this is less important. Talk about the audiences for the writing and, where possible, ask the children to read pieces aloud.

Explain that the children are going to display their pieces of writing and will need to write a description of their collection so that others will be able to know what is included. They might write one or two sentences about each passage, describing what it is, who wrote it, who it was written for and why it was written. For example:

This is a shopping list written by my dad. He wrote it for himself so that he would remember what he needed to buy at the supermarket.

This is a letter from my Aunt Sue. She wrote it to me to thank me for sending her a birthday present.

This is an invitation to Stephen's party. He wrote it and sent it to me to ask me if I would like to come to his party.

A collection of your own, suitably labelled and displayed, might provide a good example for the children to follow.

When the children have completed their writing ask them to mount their pieces of writing, together with their examples, on a large piece of sugar paper which will be put on the wall for others to see.

Suggestion(s) for extension

Children could attempt their own pieces of writing on the same lines as some of their examples. For example, a letter, an invitation or an advertisement could be produced.

Suggestion(s) for support

Some children might work in pairs to produce joint displays.

Assessment opportunities

Note the children's abilities to appreciate that there are many different types of writing and note the accuracy of their descriptions of their collections.

Display ideas

Collections can be displayed on large pieces of sugar paper so that everyone can see the range of writing.

Other aspects of the English PoS covered

Reading – 1c; 3b.

OPPOSITES

To demonstrate understanding of opposites and an ability to use sentence writing within a structured activity.

†† *Whole class or group, working together initially and then in pairs.*

⏲ *One hour.*

Key background information

This activity is designed to develop children's vocabularies by encouraging them to consider words with opposite meanings or antonyms. After initial discussion about pairs of words with opposite meanings, the children are asked to write sentences which have opposite meanings to the ones which are presented to them.

Preparation

Prepare for the activity by writing words which have opposites on the chalkboard or on individual pieces of card. Make copies of photocopiable page 124, one for each child. Prepare a word bank of opposites for the support activity.

Resources needed

A collection of words which have antonyms (see above), photocopiable page 124, chalkboard, writing materials. Dictionaries for extension activity. Word bank of opposites for support activity.

Opposites

Name _____ Date _____

▲ Look at the sentences and then try to write a sentence which means the opposite of each one.

The tall man was sitting smiling.

It was a lovely, sunny day with a clear blue sky.

David was very good at football.

The big boy was playing outside.

I was very unhappy when I lost my ballet shoes.

The winter days are short, cold and dark.

Alice hit the ball and it flew high into the air.

What to do

A starting point for this activity might be discussion of a child's disagreement which degenerates into 'Can!, Can't!, Did!, Didn't!' and so on. From this, children can be shown how lots of words have antonyms. Mention words such as 'good' and 'bad', 'happy' and 'sad', 'big' and 'small'. Then offer one word and ask the children to tell you its opposite. You might try the following: 'light', 'fast', 'ugly', 'heavy', 'on', 'up', 'in', 'over', 'late', 'hot' and 'hard'.

When the children have understood the concept of opposites, try writing some sentences on the board and ask them to think of sentences which would have the opposite meaning. The following examples might be used:

The tall man was very happy because he had won £10.
The little girl switched the light off and went downstairs.

When the children are ready to attempt more independent

work, show them the photocopiable sheet and give out copies of it. Ask them to think carefully about the sentences they might write with opposite meanings to those shown. Encourage them to experiment and reassure them that there are different ways in which their sentences could be written. In some of the sentences the changing of one word would be sufficient to change the entire meaning of the sentence while in others two, three or even four words might be changed. Encourage children to discuss the sentences with a partner and decide between them on ways of changing them.

Suggestion(s) for extension
Children could make their own collections of opposites using dictionaries or with the help of parents or guardians at home. A class list could be compiled and might form part of a word bank.

Suggestion(s) for support
Provide a word bank of opposites which the children can draw upon for ideas and for help with spellings.

Assessment opportunities
Look for evidence that children are able to construct sentences using capital letters and full stops and note their abilities to make interesting vocabulary choices. Note, in particular, their abilities to understand the concept of an antonym.

Opportunities for IT
The children could use an electronic thesaurus to help them search for opposites. They could also produce a class list of opposites using a word processor, with each child adding one or two of their favourites to the list.

Display ideas
A display of opposites could be made which included pairs of words written and illustrated by the children.

Other aspects of the English PoS covered
Speaking and listening – 3b.
Reading – 2b.

Reference to photocopiable sheet
Photocopiable page 124 provides example of sentences which can be rewritten to have an opposite meaning.

HOMONYMS

To show increased knowledge of words and their meanings and improved spelling of common homonyms.

†† *Work as a group, followed by paired or individual work.*

⏱ *Up to one hour initially, followed by work at home and in school.*

Key background information
'Homonym' has come to be the general term for a word which has the same sound and perhaps the same spelling as another, but a different meaning. Such words are also sometimes referred to as 'homophones'. In this activity children are presented with words which sound the same, but have different spellings and different meanings.

Preparation
Prepare a selection of homonyms to use as an introduction to the concept. Make copies of photocopiable page 125, one for each child.

Name _____ Homonyms Date _____
▲ Can you choose the right word to put into each sentence?
1 We had to .... a long time for the bus. (wait/weight)
2 He did not .... the answer to the question. (no/know)
3 Indra thought she .... a ghost when she woke up. (saw/sore)
4 Steven had .... T-shirts. (for/four)
▲ Now read the story and see if you can choose the right words to fill in the spaces.
It was a dark and windy .... (knight/night). The Hobbs family had decided to .... (sale/sail) to France in the dark. James and Kate sat in the cabin and .... (ate/eight) some biscuits and drank cocoa.
Suddenly .... (there/their) was a loud crashing sound. The children ran up the .... (sea/see) what had happened. 'I must have fallen asleep!' called their .... (stares/stairs) to the deck to (seem/seam) to have hit a rock.' .... (farther/father). 'We ....
Just then .... (there/their) mother climbed over the side of the boat and on to the deck. She was soaking wet. 'It's all .... (write/right),' she said. 'The boat doesn't have a .... (whole/hole) in it and anyway, we will be on the .... (beech/beach) soon.'
The sun rose and the children saw that there were houses nearby. 'Now there is just one thing to worry about,' said .... (their/there) father. 'Are we in France or are we in England?'

Resources needed

List of homonyms, photocopiable page 125, card, A2 paper, box for 'Snap' cards, chalkboard, writing and drawing materials.

What to do

Present the children with a selection of homonyms and ask them to offer sentences which include each word. Talk about the ways in which the words look or sound the same but have different meanings. You can use the following pairs of words as a good starting point:

see/sea	sail/sale	ate/eight
dear/deer	buy/by	him/hymn
missed/mist	peace/piece	son/sun
wood/would	their/there	steal/steel

Ask the children if they can think of any others. Suggest that they could try to find more homonyms at home, perhaps with the help of their family. Encourage them to bring their collections to school, but tell them that they must be able to read the words and should be able to tell others what they mean.

Discuss the words which the children have found and write examples on a sheet of A2 paper for display. The display can be referred to regularly to highlight spellings and may also act as a word bank. Ask the children to pair the words and make sets out of card. The cards can be kept in a box so that children can play a form of Snap with them. In order to win a pair of cards they have to give a sentence with each of the words in it.

To conclude the activity, give out one copy of photocopiable page 125 to each child and ask the children to complete the sheet, inserting the appropriate words in the spaces.

Suggestion(s) for extension

The children could be asked to write sentences for each other, each sentence offering a choice of two homonyms to place in a space where there is a missing word. Having completed the photocopiable sheet, they will be able to do this more confidently.

Suggestion(s) for support

The children could be asked to draw pictures to go with the most common homonyms in order to remind themselves of which word is appropriate to which situation.

Assessment opportunities

Look for evidence that children are able to spell commonly occurring simple homonyms.

Opportunities for IT

The children could use a word processor to produce a class list of homonyms. If they have access to a talking word processor they could experiment with the sounds of words that they think may be homonyms.

Display ideas

A display of the children's individual collections of homonyms could be placed around the A2 sheet of homonyms. The illustrations for the homonyms that children have drawn in the support activity could be made into a class chart of the most common homonyms and used as a reference point for all pupils.

Other aspects of the English PoS covered

Speaking and listening – 3b.
Reading – 2b.

Reference to photocopiable sheet

Photocopiable page 125 enables the children to use their knowledge gained from the activity on homonyms to choose the correct words to complete a selection of sentences and a story.

ADVERB POEMS

To understand the function of adverbs and to produce descriptive and poetic writing.

†† *Whole class and individual work.*

🕐 *At least one hour.*

Previous skills/knowledge needed

Children need to know what a verb is and they need to have read some nursery rhymes and poems.

Key background information

In this activity the children will learn that an adverb is a word which describes a verb and that adverbs often end with the suffix 'ly', for example: 'She ran *quickly*.'

Preparation

Prepare ten slips of paper and write an adverb on each one. Prepare a selection of photographs or pictures from magazines of animals in movement. Put aside one of the photographs to use in the activity and display the other photographs prominently around the classroom. Under each photograph write a one-sentence caption describing what the animal is doing. For example, 'The tiger snarls', 'The snake slithers', 'The monkey chatters' and so on.

Resources needed

Photographs of animals or pictures of animals cut out of magazines, captions for the photographs (see 'Preparation'). Slips of paper to write adverbs on, chalkboard, writing materials. Drawing materials for the support activity.

What to do

Explain to the children what an adverb is and write some examples on the board. Ask them to suggest others. Once the children have grasped the concept, introduce the 'In the manner of the word' game. Give ten individuals the slips of paper with the adverbs written on them. In turn, these pupils come out to the front of the class. The others can ask them to run, walk, jump, crawl, laugh and so on (anything, as long as it is a verb!) in the manner of the word. The object of the exercise is to guess the adverb.

Show the children the animal picture you have set aside. Invite them to suggest adverbs to describe the way the animal is moving. Ask each of the children to choose one of the photographs displayed around the room. They must now write an 'adverb list poem' about their chosen animal. The poem ends with the caption attached to the photograph. The child's task is to think of at least five suitable adverbs which describe the animal's movement and which lead up to the final line. Each adverb is placed on a separate line. For example:

Slowly
Silently
Threateningly
Hungrily
Angrily
The snake slithers.

Suggestion(s) for extension

The children can be introduced to other poetic structures and devices by selecting their adverbs so that the first letter of the words spells the name of the animal (acrostics) or by choosing adverbs which begin with the same letter (alliteration). The 'adverb list poem' could be developed to incorporate work on similes by asking the pupils to follow each adverb with a dash and the phrase 'like a...': for example, 'Silently – like a ghost'.

The children could be asked to explain why they felt that their chosen adverb went with a specific verb.

Suggestion(s) for support

Some children will grasp the function of adverbs more easily if they are referred to as 'ly' words. 'In the manner of the word' game could be played in pairs or small groups. Composing the 'adverb list poem' as an acrostic may prove easier for some children because it provides them with a clearer structure within which to work. The poems could be shaped like the animal concerned and illustrated.

Assessment opportunities

Children's understanding of the function of adverbs can be assessed through their 'adverb list poems', especially if they complete the extension activity which invites them to explain why a particular adverb was chosen.

Opportunities for IT

Children could write their adverb poems using a word processor. The adverbs could be highlighted in italics or bold, or written in a different font to make them stand out.

Display ideas

Display the 'adverb list poems', together with the photographs which inspired them. Design a humorous logo for the display, showing a figure representing an adverb supporting a figure which represents a verb.

Other aspects of the English PoS covered

Speaking and listening – 3b.
Reading – 1a, c, d; 2b.

SUBJECT–VERB AGREEMENT

To demonstrate an understanding of the concept of subject–verb agreement in writing.

†† *Individual and small group work.*

⏱ *One hour.*

Previous skills/knowledge needed

Children should be familiar with the structure of simple written sentences. For the extension activity, they will also need some awareness of the basic conventions of letter writing.

Key background information

There is a danger of 'blinding with science' when discussing rules of grammar with children of this age. Children can grasp a concept implicitly without necessarily being able to analyse its technical details. As the class teacher, you are the best judge of how much (if any) explicit technical information about the concept of subject–verb agreement your pupils could usefully absorb. Keep it simple: the children can return to these issues at a deeper level later in their school careers! One useful guideline is to ask the children to imagine that they have to try to explain the principles of subject–verb agreement to a younger brother or sister who does not understand how the rules work.

Simple written sentences consist of a subject, verb and object. For example: Sue *(subject)* kicks *(verb)* the ball *(object)*. The subject of a simple written sentence is either a noun or a pronoun. In the example given above, the noun 'Sue' could have been replaced by the pronoun 'she'.

Name _____

Subject–verb agreement

Date _____

▲ Look at the example of a three-year-old child talking to her father and try to identify her mistakes. Write what Sarah should have said on each line.

Sarah: Jane be over there, Daddy.

_____

Father: Oh, yes, I can see her.

Sarah: Why did her go there, Daddy?

_____

Father: She went to get a cake.

Sarah: You given her one?

_____

Father: Yes, I did.

Sarah: And Jane comed for a cake.

_____

The tense of a verb indicates the time at which the action takes place. There are two basic tense forms in English: the *present* and the *past*. Verbs which indicate the past tense by adding the suffix '-ed' to the verb stem are known as *regular* verbs. For example: 'walk, walked'.

Verbs which indicate the past tense by changing the vowel of the verb stem are known as *irregular* verbs. For example: 'run, ran'.

Why did her go there, Daddy?

Preparation
Decide how much technical information about subject–verb agreement you wish to impart to your pupils during this activity. Make copies of photocopiable page 126, one for each child.

Resources needed
Photocopiable page 126, writing materials. Cassette player and blank cassette for extension activity.

What to do
Ask the children if they have any amusing stories to tell about younger brothers, sisters or cousins who are learning to talk. Have their own parents told them about things they used to say when they were little? Try to use these anecdotes to help the children understand that all forms of communication have to conform to rules if people are to understand each other. We are amused by the mistakes made by little children who are learning to talk because they break these rules in unintentionally humorous ways.

Explain to the pupils that young children acquire language gradually. Show them the transcript of the dialogue between the three-year-old Sarah and her father on photocopiable page 126. Read the part of the father and ask one of the children to read Sarah's part. Ask the children to identify the points in the dialogue where Sarah breaks the rules and to suggest what the grammatically correct version should be. Ask the children to write the grammatically correct version of each of Sarah's statements underneath her version.

Suggestion(s) for extension
Children could go on to look at sentences in which the verb has been missed out, such as in the examples below:

The doll _____ a red dress and blue shoes.

Jack _____ his dinner slowly.

The cat _____ up the tree.

Children should be told that there are many possibilities for verbs to complete the sentences. The important thing is to make sure the sentences make sense grammatically.

They could go on to make up sentences of their own with missing words and give these to friends to complete.

Suggestion(s) for support
Spend time working orally with children and asking them to spot your deliberate mistakes and to suggest correct alternatives. Begin with simple, but obvious examples such as:

I runned up the hill.

Lisa wented home.

Noel eated his dinner.

It may be that children use some of the incorrect versions in their own speech. In that case, it may be necessary to offer two versions of the sentences, one correct and one incorrect, and ask them to choose which one to use.

When children begin to show confidence in identifying errors and offering correct verb forms, help them to complete sentences which require a verb, such as:

William _____ his tea.

Usha _____ and hurt her leg.

Richard _____ a car.

Simon _____ out of petrol.

Assessment opportunities
Look for evidence that children are able to recognise incorrect or inappropriate verb forms and rewrite them correctly.

Display ideas
The A4 sheets completed as part of the main activity could make a colourful display on the theme of language acquisition.

Other aspects of the English PoS covered
Speaking and listening – 1a, c; 2b; 3a.
Reading – 1a; 2b.

Reference to photocopiable sheet
Photocopiable page 126 provides an example of a young child's speech. The children write a grammatically correct version of Sarah's speech on the lines provided.

SUPER SAL

To write a story with a clear beginning, middle and end, demonstrating the ability to use appropriate punctuation, spelling and presentational skills.

†† *Whole class or group, working individually.*

🕐 *At least one hour.*

Key background information
In this activity the children are read a short story about a character named Sally who has super powers. They are then asked to write a story about Super Sal themselves. They may create their own story or they may retell the one on the photocopiable sheets in their own words.

The activity should enable you to assess a number of aspects of the children's writing skills.

Preparation
Display a picture of Super-Sal (the children could draw her themselves) and prepare a list of unfamiliar words which the children might need such as 'disappear', 'invisible' and 'magical'. Make copies of photocopiable pages 127, 128 and 129, one for each child.

Resources needed
Picture (or pictures) of Super Sal, photocopiable pages 127, 128 and 129, writing materials, wordbooks/word banks.

What to do

Read the story on photocopiable pages 127 and 128 to the children and discuss it in detail. Talk to them about Sally's magical powers and draw their attention to some of the words which are used in the story.

Explain to the children that they may write their own story about Super Sal and discuss with them possible audiences for their writing. These might include children in a different class, parents or the whole school who would see a display or hear the stories read aloud in an assembly.

Talk with the children about planning their stories and show them how they could make notes to show what would happen at the beginning, middle and end.

When the children are ready to begin work ask them to try to be as accurate as they can with spelling and to consider carefully when they should use full stops and other punctuation, but explain that you want them to show you how well they can work on their own, so they should only ask for your help if it is really necessary. Any wordbooks, word banks or other resources which are normally available may still be used, but the children should be encouraged to use these independently.

It is important that the children feel that their work is valued and there should be time set aside for reading work aloud to share it with the class.

Suggestion(s) for extension

Some children may wish to write further stories about Super Sal or create their own superhuman characters and write about them.

Suggestion(s) for support

Children who experience difficulty in creating their own story might retell the story on the photocopiable sheets in their own words. Those who normally use the word processor or concept keyboard should be allowed to continue to do so.

Assessment opportunities

The activity should enable you to look at a range of aspects of writing at Key Stage 1. Particular attention should be given to the children's abilities to spell common words accurately, punctuate their writing, make appropriate use of capital letters and demonstrate an understanding of subject–verb agreement. Note, too, their abilities to plan, review and organise their writing and to write with fluency and accuracy.

The activity is not designed to test the children's memories of the story.

Display ideas

The children's stories could be displayed, together with pictures of Super Sal. Alternatively, they could be put into a class book. The stories might be read aloud in assembly as part of a theme about 'heroes'.

Other aspects of the English PoS covered

Speaking and listening – 1a, c.
Reading – 1a, b, c, d.

Reference to photocopiable sheets

Photocopiable pages 127 and 128 provide a story on which the activity is based. Photocopiable page 129 is a language study assessment sheet for your own use.

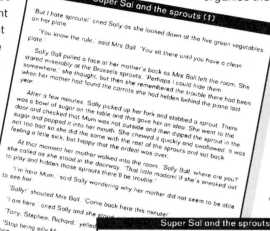

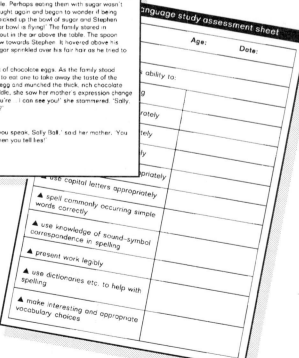

Imaginative writing

In this chapter activities range from those which encourage vocabulary extension through simple sentence writing to more sophisticated poetry and story writing.

The activities are intended to capitalise on children's developing imaginations as they gain greater experience of literature and the possibilities for written expression. Many of the activities relate to the children's everyday experiences, but others require a willing suspension of 'disbelief' on the part of the children.

At Key Stage 1 many children are beginning to understand the differences between written and spoken language. The extension of a range of audiences should allow them to appreciate that different styles of writing are required in different circumstances.

Some of the activities involve the children in planning and reviewing their writing, as well as exploring the nature of story structure. This emphasis on looking at the ways in which writing may be organised should enable the children to see themselves as authors who have a range of writing strategies at their disposal. To this end, this section also includes activities which are based upon published stories and poems. The value of providing examples of good literature cannot be overemphasised, since exposure to high-quality writing provides children with opportunities to see what is possible in writing.

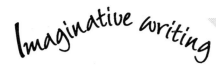

PICTURES OF PEOPLE

To make use of adjectives in descriptive writing.
†† *Whole class or group, working individually or in pairs.*
🕐 *One hour.*

Key background information

Children's early writing often includes limited use of adjectives. This activity is designed to focus attention on the function of adjectives in making writing more interesting to read. The children are presented with pictures of people who have different expressions on their faces. They are asked to name each person and describe what he or she might be like.

Preparation

Make a collection of pictures and photographs of people who have different expressions on their faces. Make copies of photocopiable page 130, one for each child or pair.

Resources needed

Photographs cut out of magazines and newspapers, lists of characteristics, lists of names (these may be found in some dictionaries), photocopiable page 130, chalkboard, writing materials.

What to do

Show the children the pictures you have collected from magazines and ask them to tell you about the people and what they might be like. Talk about possible names for the people and write some of the children's suggestions on the board. With the children, make up sentences which include a name and a description of the person for a few of the photographs. An example could be: 'Mr Gregory Brown has a long nose, a round face and very little hair. He is a kind man and he enjoys fishing and watching tennis matches.'

When the children have become more proficient at constructing the sentences orally, give them copies of photocopiable page 130 and tell them that they are going to make up sentences to describe each of the people and then write the sentences down on the photocopiable sheet. As they work, draw attention to interesting descriptions and compare their different ideas about the people. Pay particular attention to adjectives and share interesting examples by writing them on the board.

Suggestion(s) for extension

Children could write descriptions of people, and then draw pictures to accompany their writing. They could then give their descriptions, but not their pictures, to others who could try to draw pictures to go with them. The two pictures could then be compared and the written description discussed.

Suggestion(s) for support

Children who find the writing difficult could be provided with parts of sentences and be asked to complete them. For example: **Mr _____ has a _____ nose and _____ hair. He is a _____ man and he likes to _____.**

Assessment opportunities

Note children's abilities to make interesting vocabulary choices and their abilities to construct sentences.

Opportunities for IT

The children could write their descriptions using a word processor. If your school has a scanner, the pictures could be scanned and the digital versions added to the writing. Children could also use an art or drawing package to draw their own faces, which could then be added to their written work. Specific software such as *Brilliant Computing's Facemaker*, or *My World 2 Face IT*, could be used to extend this activity.

Display ideas

The pictures could be displayed on one board with the writing about each person on an adjacent board, so that children could read the writing and look at the pictures and try to match the two. This would provide an incentive for careful and accurate descriptions.

Other aspects of the English PoS covered

Speaking and listening – 1a.

Reference to photocopiable sheet

Photocopiable page 130 shows pictures of people who have a range of facial expressions. The children write sentences about the people to describe them.

I HAVE A FEELING

To make use of adjectives to describe the feel and appearance of different materials.

†† *Whole class or group, working individually or in pairs.*

🕒 *At least one hour.*

Key background information

In this activity the children use their sense of touch to explore different materials and go on to describe them both orally and in writing. The activity will enable the children to explore the use of adjectives.

Preparation

Prepare a feely box. This can be made from a cardboard box with a circular hole cut into it. The box may be covered with decorative paper. Make a collection of different materials. These might include fur, various types of cloth, cotton wool, sponge, rubber balls, fine grain sandpaper and various other items which children may safely feel.

A further collection of items should be made for each group of children who are to attempt the activity. These might be placed in a small box. Chocolate boxes are ideal.

Resources needed

Large box and small boxes with various materials inside them (see above), chalkboard, writing materials. Word lists for support activity.

What to do

Show the children the feely box and explain to them that there are many different things inside it which they will be taking turns to feel. They will not be able to see the items, so they will have to feel them very carefully if they are to work out what they might be. Before they begin, ask them to feel an item of their clothing and invite them to describe what they feel. Write some of the adjectives which they use on the board, both to provide ideas and to help with spelling

in the subsequent writing activity.

Ask the children to take turns to put a hand into the feely box and to describe the item which they feel. Explain that you do not want them to guess what the item might be just yet, but you want them to describe how it feels. Once again, write their adjectives on the board for future reference.

When the children have taken a turn at the feely box put them into groups. Explain that each group is to be given a box with different materials in it. When they begin work they will be asked not only to feel the items and describe them, but also to describe their appearance. Draw their attention to the words on the board and discuss spellings and make sure that the children understand what the words say.

Provide each child or pair with paper on which to write descriptions. These might take the form of a sentence in which the item is described using two adjectives for its feel and another two for its appearance. For example:

'The fur is soft and smooth and it looks brown and hairy.'

Ask them to work individually or in pairs to write descriptions and explain that they will be asked to read their work to the rest of the class later so that ideas may be shared. As the children work, stop them occasionally to share good ideas and to show them how to spell some of the adjectives which they are using.

At the end of the lesson ask the groups to bring out their materials and hold them up so that everyone may see them. Read out the children's descriptions and write some of their adjectives on the board. Ask the rest of the class to decide which items were being described in each case.

Suggestion(s) for extension

Some children may be able to write at greater length about the items and may include several adjectives. They could go on to describe other items around the classroom without naming them and ask other children to determine what was being described.

Suggestion(s) for support

Some children may need to be provided with a list of useful describing words from which to make selections. These should be discussed with the children before they begin work to ensure that they are able to read the words.

Assessment opportunities

Note the children's abilities to make interesting vocabulary choices and to use these appropriately. Look for evidence of a knowledge of sound–symbol correspondence where children use words which you have not provided. Where children make use of words you have written note their abilities to copy accurately.

Display ideas

Materials which have been described could be displayed, together with the children's descriptions and a collection of adjectives written on card or on strips of paper.

Other aspects of the English PoS covered

Speaking and listening – 1a, 3b.
Reading – 2b.

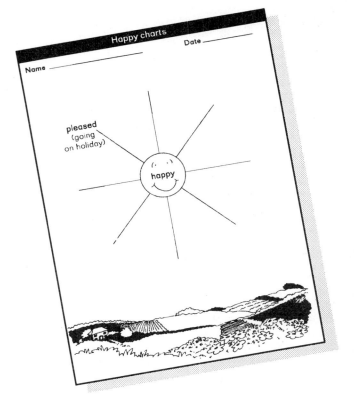

HAPPY CHARTS

To present ideas imaginatively without writing sentences and to use these as a basis for poetry or prose writing.

†† *Whole class or group, working individually or in pairs.*
⏲ *One hour.*

Key background information

This activity is intended to develop children's abilities to present writing in different ways. They are provided with the basis for a chart which has the word 'happy' in the centre. The children are asked to write at the end of each line drawn from the centre of the chart a synonym for 'happy' and then to write a short phrase next to it about something which makes them happy. The activity provides an introduction to the concept of a thesaurus and encourages children to think about synonyms.

Preparation

Make copies of photocopiable page 131, one for each child or pair.

Resources needed

Photocopiable page 131, chalkboard, writing materials. Word bank for support activity.

What to do

Draw a circle in the centre of the board and write in it the word 'sad'. Draw lines from the circle and ask the children

to think of things which mean the same as 'sad'. As they offer suggestions write these at the ends of the lines so that gradually a web appears. Next, ask them to think of things which make them sad and add their suggestions next to each synonym.

Some useful synonyms for sad which might be suggested if the children run out of ideas include: 'unhappy', 'miserable', 'sorrowful', 'disappointed' and 'sorry'.

Now explain that you want to cheer them up so they are going to think about the things which make them happy. Give out copies of photocopiable page 131 for the children to use as a starting point for their happy charts. There are lines drawn from the centre of the chart and the children

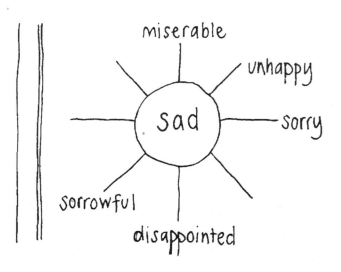

write at the end of each one a synonym for happy and then something which makes them feel happy. If they seem unable to think of many ideas make use of the class 'sad chart' and discuss opposites. Some useful synonyms for happy include 'glad', 'pleased', cheerful', 'merry', 'satisfied', 'delighted' and 'joyful'. As the children work, draw their attention to examples of interesting vocabulary choices and ideas.

Suggestion(s) for extension
Children could write sentences to describe happiness and the things which make them happy. Encourage them to make use of as many synonyms for 'happy' as possible to make their writing varied and interesting.

Suggestion(s) for support
Provide a word bank for children to draw upon when they experience difficulties with writing their ideas on the happy charts.

Assessment opportunities
Look for examples of interesting vocabulary choices and of accurate spelling where the child has used sound–symbol relationships and phonological awareness to make logical attempts at spelling unfamiliar words.

Display ideas
A class happy chart could be displayed which incorporates all of the children's synonyms for 'happy' and their ideas about what makes them happy.

Other aspects of the English PoS covered
Speaking and listening – 3b.

Reference to photocopiable sheet
Photocopiable page 131 provides an example of a 'happy chart' on which the children write synonyms for 'happy' and write about the things which make them happy.

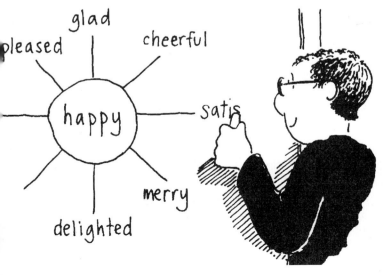

A HARVEST PRAYER

To write in response to a stimulus, showing an ability to use a prayer format.

†† *Group of children who have been asked if they would like to write prayers for harvest festival.*

🕐 *Approximately one hour.*

Previous skills/knowledge needed
Children will need to be familiar with the formats commonly used for prayers.

Key background information
In this activity children consider the things for which they are thankful at harvest time and write a prayer which could be read at a harvest festival. It may be a good idea to find out more about harvest celebrations for non-Christian faiths. The activity can be used to draw children's attention to drought and famine in other parts of the world.

Preparation
Provide examples of items which could be donated for a harvest festival.

Resources needed
Foodstuffs which can be donated for a harvest festival, writing and drawing materials.

What to do
Talk with the children about the harvest and tell them that people all over the world celebrate the time when crops are ripe and fruit is gathered. Many hold services to thank their gods for the harvest and prayers are said.

Discuss the differences between the amounts of food which we have available and the food which is available in poorer countries. Tell the children that you would like them to write prayers to express their gratitude for the food which we have to eat. Ask them to think about all of the different kinds of food which they like to eat and show them some of the items which have been donated for the harvest festival.

Ask the children what farmers need to make the harvest successful. Talk about the weather and the soil and the people who work to harvest the crops. Many children may not realise that the food which they find in tins and packets has been grown as crops or raised as animals. Talk also about the harvest from the sea and about the different countries from which we import food. The packages often provide such information.

When the children come to write their prayers ask them to start by making notes describing what they will write. They might be given a structure such as:
▲ To whom am I grateful?
▲ What am I grateful for?
▲ Why am I grateful?

▲ What would I wish for the people who do not have enough food?

If children are to end their prayers with the word 'amen' the meaning of the word ('let it be' or 'so be it') should be explained to them.

Suggestion(s) for extension
Children could write a short piece on the subject of harvest festivals and write about what makes a good harvest, or where we get our food from, or about the problems of growing crops in poorer countries.

Suggestion(s) for support
Some children may need the support of a series of unfinished sentences for their prayers with their suggested endings being written separately for them by an adult helper before the children complete the prayers. For example:

Thank you for...
We are grateful for...

The children could make use of words such as 'harvest', 'fields', 'rain', 'grow', 'sunshine', 'farmers', 'crops', 'fruit', 'vegetables' and 'corn'.

Assessment opportunities
Look for evidence that children are able to adopt an appropriate style for writing prayers and are able to read their work aloud.

Opportunities for IT
The children could use a concept keyboard with an appropriate overlay giving the beginning of the sentences. The overlay could also include a list of other words to use. The children can then create their own prayers by combining the various parts. New words could be added from the keyboard.

A similar approach could include a word-processed file prepared by you which contains the beginning of the sentences. The children could load it into the word processor and then complete the sentences with appropriate words.

Display ideas
The prayers should ideally be read aloud at a harvest assembly in order to provide a real audience for the children's writing. Copies can be displayed alongside collections of food. Where the food is to be distributed to pensioners or others, children's prayers could be written on cards to accompany the harvest gifts.

Other aspects of the English PoS covered
Speaking and listening – 1a; 2a, b.
Reading – 1a, d; 2c; 3.

A LETTER TO SANTA CLAUS

To write a letter for a 'real' audience.
✝✝ *Whole class or group, working individually.*
🕐 *One hour.*

Key background information
This activity provides an introduction to informal letter writing. Children are often asked to write to Santa Claus asking for presents. In this activity they may do this, but they are also asked to tell him what they would like other people to receive. You provide the audience and replies to letters can be provided for the children. This activity could be done as a prelude to, or a follow-up to, 'Do they know it's Christmas?' on page 107.

Preparation
Write your own letter to Santa Claus in which you ask about presents for yourself and for others. Include some questions about life in Lapland and tell Santa a little about yourself. Make copies of photocopiable page 132, one for each child or group.

Resources needed
Photocopiable page 132, writing materials, coloured pencils or felt-tipped pens for illustrations.

What to do
Talk with the children about Christmas and the presents which they and their families gave and received last year. Ask them about the things they would like to receive this year and about the things that they would like their family and friends to receive.

Read to the children your letter to Santa Claus. Explain

that they are going to write a letter to Santa Claus telling him about the presents they would like and the things they would like their family and friends to receive.

Give out the copies of photocopiable page 132 and read the letter from Santa Claus to the children, which will help them to prepare their letters by giving them initial ideas. Tell them that if they write well he may reply. Ask them to include some questions about Santa and where he lives. The children might ask about what Santa Claus does for the rest of the year. Some children may demur at the idea of Santa's existence and this will need to be dealt with sensitively so that other children are not affected.

Discuss with the children a simple layout for letter writing. This might include the child's address or the school address, the date, an introductory 'Dear Santa' and a final 'Love from...'.

The children can illustrate their finished letters before they are put into a large envelope addressed to Santa Claus. It is important that children receive a reply to their letters. This could be in the form of individual letters written by you but this could prove very time-consuming. An alternative would be to write one long letter to the whole class in which several children's questions are answered, or to word-process one letter and add touches of individuality for each child.

A letter from Santa Claus

Dear

I hope that you are well and that you are looking forward to Christmas.

I am always very busy at this time of the year. There are so many jobs to do. I have to clean and polish the sleigh and groom the reindeer. Then there are all those presents to sort out. I hardly have time to stop for something to eat. Mind you, I have been trying not to eat too much. I am beginning to get a bit too fat to get down some of the chimneys!

Have you been busy finding presents for your family? What would you like to give to them? Last year I received two hundred and fifty bottles of aftershave. I wouldn't mind, but I have a beard!

Do you know what you would like for Christmas? Perhaps you could tell me when you write to me. I would like some warm socks and some thick gloves. It's very cold sitting on that sleigh in the middle of winter!

This year I have a new reindeer. I haven't thought of a name for him yet. Do you have any ideas? I'd love to hear them if you do.

Well, I suppose I had better get back to work. Please write to me and tell me all about yourself and your family and friends. I would love to hear from you.

Merry Christmas

Santa

Internet it may be possible to send electronic versions of the children's letters to an appropriate e-mail address. You may be able to make a reciprocal arrangement with a teacher at another school who will reply to your pupils' letters so that they get an electronic reply. This style of writing is different to conventional letter writing and the children should see some examples before they start so that they may gain a simple understanding of what happens when they send their e-mail.

Display ideas

Letters should be 'sent' to Santa, so they should not be displayed if the children are to feel that they are writing for a real audience. Santa's reply could be displayed prominently for children to read. A tailor's dummy dressed as Santa could be the focal point for a Christmas display which included Santa's reply.

Other aspects of the English PoS covered

Speaking and listening – 1a.
Reading – 1c, d.

Reference to photocopiable sheet

Photocopiable page 132 provides a letter from Santa Claus to initiate the activity and includes questions to stimulate the children's ideas.

Suggestion(s) for extension

Some children may wish to write to Santa Claus again, in which case a correspondence could be set up.

Suggestion(s) for support

Some children could copy a letter and, with the help of an adult, add personal details in spaces left for the purpose.

Assessment opportunities

Note the children's abilities to set out letters correctly and to take into account the reader in what they write.

Opportunities for IT

If your school has access to the

THE MONSTER

To produce descriptive and commentary writing.

†† *Whole class or group, working individually or in pairs.*

🕐 *At least one hour. The work may be spread over two days with drawing on one day and writing on another.*

Key background information

This activity might be attempted in conjunction with work on dinosaurs or on plants and animals. Young children are often fascinated by dinosaurs and large creatures. In this activity they are encouraged to draw and describe a monster of their own creation.

Preparation

Provide plenty of pictures of large animals including dinosaurs and, perhaps, mythical creatures such as griffins, wyverns, and the Minotaur. Pictures purporting to show the Loch Ness monster might also be used. Models of dinosaurs are often owned by children and they could be asked to bring these to school. Look for examples of descriptions of monsters from fiction. These might include *The Iron Man* by Ted Hughes (Faber, 1989) and descriptions of Frankenstein's monster in Mary Shelley's *Frankenstein* (Penguin, 1994).

Resources needed

Pictures of monsters, examples of descriptions of monsters from fiction (see above), dinosaur models (optional), writing and drawing materials, scrap paper.

What to do

Talk with the children about the pictures (and models) of monsters and ask them to tell you which ones they recognise and to give you any information which they have about them.

Explain that the children are going to invent a monster of their own which they will first draw and then describe. They could combine the features of different creatures, or they could invent a completely new monster. Let them try out their ideas on scrap paper before they produce a final version.

When the children have drawn their monsters, ask them to choose names for them and write about them. Ask them to write about the monsters' appearance, what the monsters eat, where they live, what they do during the day and the night and any other interesting features such as what sort of temperament the monsters have. Encourage the use of interesting vocabulary to describe the creatures and tell the children that their writing will be displayed near, but not next to, their pictures, so that other people will be able to read about each one and try to identify the monster the writing describes.

As the children work, look for opportunities to extend vocabulary choices by offering suggestions and by reading to the children from the books which have examples of descriptions of creatures (see 'Preparation').

Suggestion(s) for extension

Children could go on to write stories about their creatures, incorporating the features of the monsters that they have depicted in the main activity.

Suggestion(s) for support

Children could work with an adult to make a list of the features of their monsters and then be helped to include these in sentences written about the monster.

Assessment opportunities

Look for evidence that children are able to organise their writing and make imaginative vocabulary choices.

Opportunities for IT

Children could use a word processor to write and redraft their monster writing. They could also use an art package to draw and print out their own monster picture.

Display ideas

Pictures of monsters and written descriptions of them can be displayed on the same board, but with each child's writing placed away from his or her picture, so that others can read the descriptions and try to identify the accompanying pictures.

Other aspects of the English PoS covered

Speaking and listening – 1c.

THE FANTASTIC MACHINE

To use captions and descriptive writing.
†† *Whole class or group, working individually or in pairs.*
🕐 *One hour.*

Key background information
In this activity children are asked to draw an imaginary machine and describe what it can do and what function each different part performs. The machines will be labelled and children will be encouraged to make use of adjectives and adverbs in their descriptive work.

Preparation
Find photographs of machines and, if possible, a video extract of machines at work.

Resources needed
Roald Dahl's *Charlie and the Chocolate Factory* (Puffin, 1994), pictures of machinery, video extract of machines at work, (optional), television, writing and drawing materials. LEGO and information books for extension activity.

What to do
Talk with the children about machines and their functions. If you have managed to obtain a video extract of a working machine show this to the children. Read extracts from Roald Dahl's *Charlie and the Chocolate Factory* and talk about the machines in Mr Wonka's factory. Ask the children what

sorts of things they would like machines to do for them. The discussion may turn to robots, in which case the subsequent writing could focus upon these if children wish.

Explain to the children that they are going to design a machine on paper and describe what it does. The machine will be labelled with the names of the components and the children will then need to describe the function of each part.

Discuss with the children the ways in which they might describe each function, using adverbs to tell the reader how the machine operates and adjectives to describe the parts. This may provide an opportunity to discuss with the children the functions of adverbs and adjectives. The pictures of machinery from *Charlie and the Chocolate Factory* might be used in conjunction with the text as a stimulus to oral descriptions.

Suggestion(s) for extension
Children could go on to use LEGO or other materials to make machines. Some might use information books to find out more about machines.

Suggestion(s) for support
Children who might experience difficulties with the writing could be grouped together and asked to brainstorm ideas for verbs which show what the different parts of machines do. These could be recorded on a large piece of paper which could act as a word bank.

Assessment opportunities
Look for evidence that children are able to relate their writing to their drawings and note their abilities to make use of adverbs and adjectives to enhance their descriptive work.

Display ideas
Pictures of real machines could be displayed, together with the children's pictures, and descriptions could be placed next to the appropriate parts of the machines.

Other aspects of the English PoS covered
Speaking and listening – 1a; 2b.

THE SCARECROW

To produce note-making and sentence writing in an imaginative piece of writing.
†† *Whole class or group, working individually or in pairs.*
🕐 *One hour initially, but this is an ongoing activity.*

Key background information
Children's early writing is often egocentric, but in this activity children write sentences from the point of view of a scarecrow. They will draft their work into sentences after making notes.

Preparation

Teach the children the song 'The Scarecrow' from *Oranges and Lemons*, compiled by Karen King (Oxford University Press, 1995). Talk about and/or read one of the *Worzel Gummidge* stories by Barbara Euphan Todd (Puffin, 1989). Make copies of photocopiable page 133, one for each child or pair.

Resources needed

Wood for a frame, clothes for dressing the scarecrow and material for the head – this could be an old cushion, a ball, a balloon or a pumpkin. Books (see above). Photocopiable page 133, chalkboard, writing materials.

What to do

Talk with the children about scarecrows and ask them if they know what they are used for. Explain that a local farmer or gardener needs a realistic scarecrow and that they have been asked to make one for him or her. If possible, arrange for a farm or garden to be visited to see a scarecrow. Alternatively, place the scarecrow that the children make in the school grounds.

Provide the materials you have collected and help a group of children to make a scarecrow. When the scarecrow is finished ask the children to think of a name for it. Take the children to the site where the scarecrow is to be placed and talk with them about the things the scarecrow will be able to see and hear. Ask them to jot down notes on the scarecrow's surroundings. When the children return to the classroom ask them to complete the sentences on photocopiable page 133.

The children's sentences should be read aloud and discussed. Interesting vocabulary choices could be written on the board and a word bank might be developed.

Suggestion(s) for extension

Children could write diaries for the scarecrow detailing what he or she has seen and heard (and even smelled!) each day. Stories could be written about the scarecrow moving and meeting other scarecrows.

Suggestion(s) for support

The word bank compiled in the main activity will provide support for those children who need help with spellings.

Assessment opportunities

Note the children's abilities to complete sentences and their success in composing their own sentences and their abilities to write consistently from another's point of view.

Opportunities for IT

The children could use a word processor to write and draft their work. A prepared file could include the beginning of the scarecrow sentences. The children could then load these into the word processor and complete them.

Display ideas

The scarecrow could be brought into the classroom and the children's writing displayed next to it.

Other aspects of the English PoS covered

Speaking and listening – 2c.
Reading – 1c, d; 2b.

Reference to photocopiable sheet

The beginnings of sentences set out on photocopiable page 133 will allow the children to focus on specific details when describing their scarecrow. They can use the notes which they made earlier on the scarecrow's environment.

TONGUE-TWISTERS

To demonstrate a growing awareness of sound–symbol relationships and phonological patterns through an imaginative writing activity.

†† *Whole class or group, working in pairs.*

⏱ *One hour.*

Previous skills/knowledge needed
Children will need to have some understanding of sound–symbol correspondence. This might be developed through games such as 'I-spy'.

Key background information
A knowledge of the sound–symbol relationships of initial letter sounds is important as children develop their reading skills. In this activity they produce pieces of imaginative writing which focus attention on these sounds.

Preparation
Find examples of tongue-twisters.

Resources needed
Examples of tongue-twisters, dictionaries, chalkboard, writing materials.

What to do
Read some tongue-twisters to the children. You could either read to the children, or write on the board, the examples below:

Six sizzling sausages sat still on a saucer.
Five fat frogs fought furiously for food
Happy Harry hit his hand hard with a hammer
Big boys began boxing bananas on a boat.

Make up some more by starting them yourself and asking the children to add to them. Talk to the children about the sorts of words which could appear in the tongue-twisters and make lists on the board. When children make inappropriate suggestions, explain why the words cannot be used and ask for alternatives which have the right beginnings.

When the children seem to have understood the concept of tongue-twisters ask them to write some of their own. Make dictionaries available to those who need them. (For this activity the children focus on alliterative tongue-twisters only.) It may be a good idea to have everyone start with the same letter so that children's work may be used to provide examples. In order to reinforce learning and to help those who experience difficulties it is a good idea to show the children regularly the work that others have been doing.

Suggestion(s) for extension
Children who cope well with the main activity might be asked to make tongue-twister acrostics with a tongue-twisting sentence for each letter of a word. For example:

Sun, sand and sea
Use of umbrellas unusual
Mild midsummer
Mellow mood
Endless, easy evenings
Rain rarely reaches us

Wind whistles wildly
Icicles in icy igloos
Nasty nights nearing now
Train travel terrible
Every evening empty
Rains regularly

Suggestion(s) for support
Some children may need help from lists of words beginning with the same letter. The lists may be created through brainstorming sessions with the children. Simple dictionaries may be used too.

Assessment opportunities
Note the children's abilities to relate sounds to symbols in their writing. Note incorrect but plausible attempts at spelling which suggest that understanding is developing.

Opportunities for IT
Children could use a word processor to write, draft and print their tongue-twisters. If the word processor has a speech facility the children could listen to their work as it develops. They could also make use of the dictionary attached to many word processors to find other appropriate words.

Display ideas
Tongue-twisters could be displayed on a large board with sections for each initial letter or initial blend or digraph.

Other aspects of the English PoS covered
Speaking and listening – 3b.
Reading – 2b.

FAMOUS ARTISTS

To produce writing in response to a stimulus.
✝✝ *Whole class or group, working in pairs.*
🕐 *One hour.*

Previous skills/knowledge needed

Children need to have spent time looking at paintings and talking about them.

Key background information

This activity is designed to develop children's writing in response to a stimulus. The children are provided with pictures which they look at carefully and write about. The writing will be both descriptive and creative, since the children are asked to write about what they can see and also what they feel when they look at the pictures.

Preparation

Choose one particular artist, or a theme comprising work by various artists, and collect a variety of relevant pictures. Picture postcards may be bought from art galleries. Books of works by famous artists can often be bought very cheaply from bookshops which specialise in remaindered stock. These may be cut up. Choose one large picture suitable for showing to the whole class.

Resources needed

Examples of paintings on a theme or by a particular artist, including one large picture to show to the whole class (see above), writing and drawing materials.

What to do

Look at the large picture you have chosen and encourage the children to talk about it in detail. Discuss the colours, shapes and the content. Talk about the background and the foreground and use some of the terms to form a word bank on the board. Explain that the artist uses his or her imagination as well as paint to produce a picture. Ask the children what the picture makes them think of, and encourage them to put themselves in the picture and imagine what it must have been like to be in the picture that the artist painted.

Provide each pair of children with a picture and ask them to make notes on what they can see and what the picture makes them feel. Use the notes as a starting point for a poem or a piece of descriptive writing. Encourage the children to choose suitable adjectives to describe what they can see and make use of their examples to share ideas with the rest of the class or group.

Suggestion(s) for extension

The children could attempt their own paintings, using aspects of the pictures which they have described. They could then describe, in writing, the features of their own pictures.

Suggestion(s) for support

Children who find the writing difficult could be given pictures with small Post-it notes placed next to key features with the names of the features written on them. These could be removed as the child writes about the picture.

Assessment opportunities

Note the children's abilities to make imaginative vocabulary choices and to organise their work carefully.

Opportunities for IT

If your school has access to a CD-ROM with pictures on it the images could be saved from the CD-ROM and placed into a word processor. This would enable the children to write their descriptions underneath the picture. Pictures might also be downloaded from the Internet, or scanned from books or postcards.

Display ideas

Display the children's paintings and poems, together with the famous paintings.

Other aspects of the English PoS covered

Speaking and listening – 1c.

PLANNING A STORY

To organise and plan writing through analysis of a well-known story.
✝✝ *Whole class or group, working individually or in pairs.*
🕐 *At least one hour.*

Previous skills/knowledge needed

The children should have had experience of a wide range of stories, especially fairy tales.

Key background information

Fairy stories may have many different versions. This is because they are often passed on through generations and are adapted by different storytellers. Children may know of different versions of the two stories referred to in this activity. The activity requires children to determine the structure of a well-known story. The activity can be developed further by asking children to plan their own stories, using a structure similar to that which they have identified in the well-known story.

Preparation
Find a copy of Roald Dahl's *Revolting Rhymes* (Picture Puffin, 1984) or a similar retelling of a traditional story. Make copies of photocopiable page 134, one for each child.

Resources needed
Roald Dahl's *Revolting Rhymes*, photocopiable page 134, writing and drawing materials.

What to do
Ask the children to tell you the story of Cinderella. Do this as a whole class and lead the children through the story if necessary. Next, read Roald Dahl's *Revolting Rhymes* version of Cinderella to the class. Compare Dahl's version with the children's versions of the story. Ask them to talk about the beginning, middle and end of the story. What did they like or dislike about Dahl's ending?

Explain to the children that stories have a beginning, a middle and an end. Make sure that the children are familiar with the story of *Goldilocks and the Three Bears*. Give out the copies of photocopiable page 134 and ask the children to try to answer the questions in the boxes provided. Discuss the different plans that the children have produced. Talk with them about the key events which they have identified. Some children may suggest that there are more than three. Discuss this with the whole group. Provide spellings on the board of

any words which cause the children problems.

Finally, read Roald Dahl's version of Goldilocks and ask the children to compare it with their own versions.

Suggestion(s) for extension
The children could use the format of photocopiable page 134 to plan a story of their own. They may have ideas themselves or it may be necessary to discuss possible starting points with them.

Suggestion(s) for support
It will be necessary to read the questions to the children. Children's responses may take the form of emergent writing, which can then be discussed and rewritten with the help of an adult.

Assessment opportunities
Look for understanding of story structure where children have attempted emergent writing. Look for evidence of correct letter formation.

Other aspects of the English PoS covered
Speaking and listening – 1a.
Reading – 1a.

Reference to photocopiable sheet
Photocopiable page 134 provides a structure for children to use when analysing a well-known story and may also be used as an aid to planning independent story writing.

A CLASS TRIP
To produce narrative writing in response to listening to a story related to an educational visit.
†† *Whole class or group, working individually.*
🕐 *One hour.*

Key background information
This activity is designed to prepare the children for a class trip and to interest them in the place they are to visit. The activity may be used as the first of a series related to an educational visit. Children's early story writing often includes frequent reference to friends. This activity allows for this.

Preparation
Prepare a story which you will tell the children about a trip to the place which you are going to visit. Look for lots of

opportunities to mention the children by name and to include information about the venue. Photocopiable page 135 includes possible prompts and ideas for including the children in the story.

Resources needed
Photocopiable page 135, postcards and photographs, card, chalkboard, writing materials.

What to do
Tell the children a story about their forthcoming visit. You could use the photocopiable page as an example of a story about a school trip. The story can be based on the itinerary, with references to the children made at each stage. Show them postcards and photographs as you do so and have words on the board or on card. Recap regularly and ask the children who have been mentioned in the story to remind the class of what they did.

At a suitable point ask the children to tell you what might happen next and incorporate their ideas into the story. Eventually, the children can be asked to continue the story themselves in writing. At first they might make a list of the events before developing their ideas in prose. Encourage them to be imaginative in their writing by telling them that they may choose adventures for each other.

Recap regularly on the story and read the children's efforts aloud as a means of stimulating ideas.

Suggestion(s) for extension
The stories could be written in script form or notes could be made, so that they could be dramatised and performed by the children.

Suggestion(s) for support
Children could work in pairs to produce joint stories or could write with the help of an adult. A list of events in the story

A class trip
It was the day of the trip to York and everyone was looking cross. Samantha and Amrit looked at each other and sighed. Ben started to sing 'Why are we waiting', but Mrs Mitchell told him to be quiet. Everyone in the classroom was miserable because the bus was late.

Suddenly Stephen jumped up and called, 'Mrs Mitchell, it's here. I can hear it coming!'

'Quiet everyone,' said Mrs Mitchell. 'Let's listen carefully and see if Stephen is right.' Sure enough, the sound of the bus could be heard getting louder as it got nearer to the school. 'Right, Kirsty's table line up at the door please,' said Mrs Mitchell. She then asked the children from the other tables to join them and they were ready to go. At least everyone except Mike was ready. He was still looking for his notebook so Mrs Mitchell asked Ross to help him.

At last they got on the bus and Mrs Mitchell and Mr Gray, who was coming along to help, together with Joseph's mother and William's mother, counted everyone twice to make sure that no one would be left behind. Katherine had left her packed lunch in the classroom so she had to run back and get it, but the bus finally managed to leave only half an hour late. Everyone was excited and Richard and Chris, who were sitting on the back seat, began to sing.

'Not yet, not yet!' shouted Mrs Mitchell. 'You may sing on the way home. Right now you should be looking at the worksheets which I gave to you to fill in on the journey.' Lisa and Ryan stopped writing in the mist on the window and looked at their worksheets.

'I bet I can finish mine before you,' said Lisa.

'I bet you can't,' said Ryan.

'Bet I can,' said Lisa.

'No you can't,' said Ryan.

'Excuse me,' said Mr Gray, firmly. 'I think you two should stop arguing about who is going to finish first and get started!'

could be made for children to refer to. This may need to include pictures for those who experience difficulty with reading.

Assessment opportunities
Note the children's abilities to write imaginatively, basing their writing on the itinerary which has been provided for them but adapting their work to incorporate their own ideas.

Display ideas
The children's writing could be displayed alongside work done following the actual visit and children could be encouraged to read both versions and compare them.

Other aspects of the English PoS covered
Speaking and listening – 1a; 2b.

Reference to photocopiable sheet
Photocopiable page 135 provides an example of a story about a school trip in which children's names are included regularly. This may be adapted for use with your own class.

FANTASY ISLAND

To write a story in response to a stimulus.
†† *Whole class or group, working individually or in pairs.*
⊕ *One hour.*

Previous skills/knowledge needed
Children will need to understand the concept of a map.

Key background information
This activity is designed to promote story writing, following the stimulus of being shown a map of an island and photographs. The children's names feature in the story in order

to provide them with a measure of ownership of the story. The activity can be linked to the previous one, 'A class trip'.

Preparation
Cut pictures of beaches, the sea, sunsets and so on out of colour supplements or holiday brochures. Make copies of photocopiable pages 136, 137 and 138, one for each child or pair. Prepare part of a story about the children's visit to an island, or use photocopiable pages 137 and 138. Include their names in the story regularly.

Resources needed
Pictures to support a description of an island (see above), photocopiable pages 136, 137 and 138, writing materials, stiff card. Sentence bank for support activity.

What to do
Show the children the map of the island on photocopiable page 136. Discuss the different features of the island and then tell the children your prepared section of a story about their visit to the island, or use photocopiable pages 137 and 138 which have spaces where you can write the names of children in your class. You can use the photographs you have cut out of colour magazines to help to bring the story alive.

Give out the copies of photocopiable pages 137 and 138, and ask the children to finish the story you have told them. Encourage the children to feel that they may take their stories in any direction they wish. Draw their attention to the possibilities for adventure at different points on the island and discuss their ideas before they begin to write.

If children appear to be flagging, read examples of their work aloud and suggest ways in which the stories might continue, or tell them your own story.

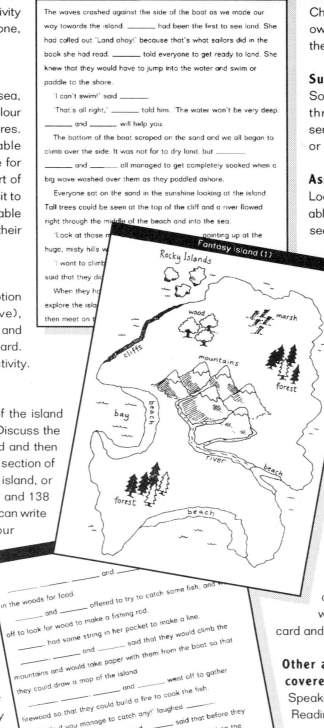

Fantasy Island (2)

The waves crashed against the side of the boat as we made our way towards the island. _____ had been the first to see land. She had called out 'Land ahoy!' because that's what sailors did in the book she had read. _____ told everyone to get ready to land. She knew that they would have to jump into the water and swim or paddle to the shore.

'I can't swim!' said _____.

'That's all right,' _____ told him. 'The water won't be very deep. _____ and _____ will help you.'

The bottom of the boat scraped on the sand and we all began to climb over the side. It was not far to dry land, but _____.

_____ and _____ all managed to get completely soaked when a big wave washed over them as they paddled ashore.

Everyone sat on the sand in the sunshine looking at the island. Tall trees could be seen at the top of the cliff and a river flowed right through the middle of the beach and into the sea.

'Look at those _____ pointing up at the huge, misty hills w_____

'I want to climb _____ said that they di_____

When they ha_____ explore the isla_____ then meet on t_____

Fantasy Island (1)

Rocky Islands
wood
marsh
mountains
forest
cliffs
bay
beach
river
beach
forest
beach

_____ and _____ in the woods for food. _____ and _____ offered to try to catch some fish, and _____ _____ off to look for wood to make a fishing rod. _____ had some string in her pocket to make a line. _____ and _____ said that they would climb the mountains and would take paper with them from the boat so that they could draw a map of the island _____, _____ and _____ went off to gather firewood so that they could build a fire to cook the fish. 'That's if you manage to catch any!' laughed _____ _____ and _____ said that before they went exploring they would go back on to the boat and drop the anchor so that it would not drift away. Everyone was excited. The children knew that they could get home safely so long as the boat was all right. Now they wanted to explore the island and look for adventure.

▲ Can you continue the story and write about the children's adventures on the island? You can use the back of this sheet.

Suggestion(s) for extension
Children could make and label their own maps and write stories about them.

Suggestion(s) for support
Some children may require support through partially completed sentences, either for the whole story or for an introduction.

Assessment opportunities
Look for evidence that children are able to use a narrative style with clear sequencing of events. Note, too, their abilities to maintain the same tense throughout the story. Children often change tenses as they write, particularly when they begin their writing in the present or future tenses.

Opportunities for IT
The children could use an art or drawing package to create their fantasy island maps to accompany their written stories.

Display ideas
The children's writing could be displayed alongside the maps they have drawn. Alternatively, a papier mâché model of the island could be made and children's writing could be mounted on stiff card and hung above it from the ceiling.

Other aspects of the English PoS covered
Speaking and listening –1a; 2a, b.
Reading – 1c.

Reference to photocopiable sheets
Photocopiable page 136 provides a map of an island with various features which can figure in the story that you tell the children (either your own story or the one provided). The children are asked to provide an ending to the accompanying story on photocopiable pages 137 and 138.

THREE WISHES

To write imaginatively in response to a stimulus.

†† *Whole class, and then individuals or pairs.*

🕐 *At least one hour.*

Key background information

A familiar theme in many children's stories is the granting of three wishes to one of the characters. In this activity the children are provided with the beginning of a story in which the characters are offered three wishes. They have to write about the wishes and may go on to write stories about what happens when the wishes are granted.

Preparation

Find examples of stories which involve the granting of wishes. These could include 'Jack One-Step' by Terry Jones in *Fairy Tales* (Puffin, 1990) and *Wishbones* by Barbara Ker Wilson and Meilo So (Frances Lincoln, 1993). Make copies of photocopiable pages 139 and 140, one copy of the story for each child.

Resources needed

Stories with a wishes theme (see above), photocopiable pages 139 and 140, chalkboard/card, writing materials. Cassette player and blank cassettes for support activity (optional).

What to do

Introduce the theme of wishes by reading the stories to the children (see 'Preparation'). Discuss the ways in which the characters in the stories use their wishes. Often the wishes are misused and the characters regret ever having had the wishes in the first place.

Talk with the children about what they would do if they were offered three wishes. You could ask them the following questions:

▲ What would you wish for yourself?
▲ What would you wish for other people?
▲ Would you use all of your wishes straight away?
▲ Would you wish to be rich?
▲ Would you wish for happiness?
▲ Would you wish to be able to do something unusual?

Introduce the children to the story on photocopiable pages 139 and 140 and let the children follow it on their copies as

Three wishes (1)

Name _____ Date _____

The wood was dark and cool after walking in the sunshine. Ella and Lewis could see shafts of light breaking through the trees. They could hear the noise of tiny animals hiding as they approached.

Soon they came to a small clearing in the woods and they stopped and looked around them. Their parents would be along in a moment. They thought about hiding and giving them a surprise. One of the trees had a large hole in its trunk which one of them would be able to squeeze into, but there would not be room for two. As they looked at the hole in the tree they suddenly realised that the woods had become quiet. The sound of animals and birdsong had gone. Ella and Lewis looked at each other and then at the wood around them. Just as Lewis was about to speak he stopped and gazed at the hole in the tree, his mouth open and his eyes wide.

'What are you two staring at?' The voice was squeaky and it belonged to a little man who had climbed out of the hole in the tree. He was unlike any person they had ever seen before. On his head he wore a green hat with a feather tucked into a band and a rim which came down over his forehead. His eyes were bright and sparkling and he had a long grey beard which covered the front of his green coat and reached the belt of his brown trousers. He wore black boots and although he looked old enough to be their grandfather he was slightly smaller than the children.

The children were too shocked to move. They went on staring at the little man hardly believing their eyes. 'Will you stop staring at me,' said the man crossly. 'Haven't you ever seen a triwishman before?'

...sh watsit?'

...shes to
...ree good
The little
...eyes do
...as really

...I've
...ld let
...tter

...gun to speak.

...wishes, what would you wish for?

2

3

▲ Can you finish the story? Imagine that you are Lewis or Ella. You can use the back of this sheet.

you read it to them. Ask them to think about what they would wish for if they were granted three wishes. Also, what would they be able to say about themselves which showed that they deserved the wishes? Talk with them about the situation in the woods and remind them about the danger of talking to strangers. (In the story the children's parents are not far away.)

Talk with the children about the name 'triwishman'. Write the word on the board or on card and ask them to look at the different parts of the word. Try to elicit from them what the word means (tri, wish, man). This work may be related to other decoding work in which children are encouraged to break longer words into syllables.

Ask the children to plan a continuation of the story. Some could do this individually, but others may need to work in pairs. Encourage them to describe people in the story. The triwishman has been described, but Ella and Lewis have not. Can the children include in their stories a description of the children's appearance?

Suggestion(s) for extension

Children could continue their stories over an extended period, turning them into booklets with illustrations if they are enjoying writing them. The stories could be read aloud to the class and to other classes.

Suggestion(s) for support

Some children could plan their stories out in pictures and write brief captions to accompany these. Alternatively, they

could jot down ideas and then tape-record stories.

Assessment opportunities

Look for evidence that children are able to plan and review their writing, can organise their writing, make use of imaginative vocabulary choices and can read their work aloud to an audience.

Opportunities for IT

Some children or pairs could write extended stories using a word processor or desktop publishing package. The children will need to save and retrieve their story each time they add to it. Pictures could be added from clip art collections, drawn using an art package or scanned from their own line drawings. Children will need to be shown how to manipulate the pictures and text to make the pages interesting. They could also add page numbers and headings, and a title or contents page.

Other aspects of the English PoS covered

Speaking and listening – 1a, c, d.
Reading – 1c, d; 2b, c; 3.

Reference to photocopiable sheets

Photocopiable pages 139 and 140 provide the beginning of a story in which two children meet someone who may grant them three wishes. The children can try to answer the accompanying questions before finishing the story themselves.

WHAT WOULD YOU BE?

To plan a story and to write in sentences through an activity based upon a published story.
†† *Whole class, followed by individual work.*
🕐 *At least one hour.*

Previous skills/knowledge needed

The children will need to be familiar with the most common colours and will need to be told a little about chameleons and their ability to change colour according to their surroundings.

Key background information

This activity is based upon the story *The Mixed-Up Chameleon* by Eric Carle (Picture Puffin, 1988) in which a chameleon decides that its life is not very exciting and wishes to change, so that it can not only adopt the colours of its surroundings but also acquire the features of other animals. The changes mean that it becomes a hybrid creature with an array of different features, but it can no longer catch flies and so ends up wishing it could be itself again. Another book with a similar theme is *Winnie the Witch* by Korky Paul and Valerie Thomas (Oxford University Press, 1989). In this story a witch has problems seeing her black cat in her black house and so changes his colour. Each time she changes the cat's colour there are problems so she finally changes him back to being black and changes the colour of her house instead.

The stories may be used as a prelude to the children being asked what they would like to be if they could choose and what they would like to change in their lives. They may go on to write about what they would like to be and could describe what they would do.

Preparation

Find a copy of Eric Carle's book or Korky Paul and Valerie Thomas's book (see above).

Resources needed

The Mixed-Up Chameleon by Eric Carle, *Winnie the Witch* by Korky Paul and Valerie Thomas, writing materials. Drawing materials for extension activity.

What to do

Read *The Mixed-Up Chameleon* and/or *Winnie the Witch* to the children. Ask them to talk about the story and discuss with them what they would like to change if they could.

Ask the children to write, in note form, their ideas for a story in which they change something about their lives. Emphasise that, at this stage, it is their ideas that are most important. They should be encouraged to experiment with spellings of less familiar words and be told that help will be given later. Point out that in the stories which you have read to them the characters revert to their original state and that they may wish to write a story in which they find that changing their lives is not such a good idea after all.

Ask the children to use their notes as the basis for a story written in sentences. Remind them that notes are temporary and that they do not have to use all of them. They may also add new ideas as they write. Read the children's work aloud as it develops and discuss the ideas and the vocabulary which they use. Words which are being used regularly, but which are being misspelled frequently, may be written on the board or on card and discussed.

Suggestion(s) for extension

Children could write their stories in book form with illustrations. Eric Carle's illustrations provide an ideal example since they are simple and colourful while still being very effective. Children could adopt a similar style in their books.

Suggestion(s) for support

Some children may need to write with a partner or with an adult helper. They could be asked to draw a series of simple pictures as a plan for their story and then be given help to add words.

Assessment opportunities

Look for evidence that children are able to plan stories in note form and then review their notes as they begin to write in sentences.

Opportunities for IT

The children could write their stories using a word processor or desktop publishing package. They could begin by typing in their notes, (this could be done in advance by another scribe), and then expanding or ordering them into a story. Remind them that they will need to save and retrieve their story each time they add to it. They could also add pictures, page numbers and headings, and a title or contents page.

Display ideas

A display of the children's writing could be put on the wall with copies of Carle's and Paul and Thomas's books placed nearby. The stories could be taped and a listening post could be placed near to the display so that children could listen to both the published and the children's stories and follow them in print.

Other aspects of the English PoS covered

Speaking and listening – 1a.
Reading – 1c, d; 2a.

💻 MY IDEAL BIRTHDAY

To produce imaginative, chronological writing in timetable form.

†† *Whole class or group, working individually.*

🕐 *One hour.*

Previous skills/knowledge needed

Pupils will need to be familiar with telling the time at a simple level.

Key background information

In this activity children produce a timetable for their ideal birthday. In order to prepare them for the activity it would be useful to link it to work on time in mathematics. You could produce a timetable for the school day showing when school starts, when assembly takes place and when playtimes and lunch-times are scheduled.

Preparation

Prepare a timetable of the school's day. Make a timetable of your own ideal birthday to show to the children. Make copies of photocopiable page 141, one for each child.

Resources needed

Timetables (see above), photocopiable page 141, word list (see 'What to do'), writing materials.

What to do

Ask the children to think about what they would really like to do on their birthdays if they could choose anything at all.

the tab key to separate the times of the day from the text. They should be discouraged from using the space bar to position the text on the page.

    7.00 am   get up and wait for the postman
    7.30 am   open my cards.

If a desktop publishing package is used, two vertical columns could be created, with the time in one and the accompanying text in the other:

| 7.00 am | get up and wait for the postman |
| 7.30 am | open my cards |

Children could use specific software such as *Banner* to create the 'Happy Birthday' banner for the class display.

Display ideas
The writing could be displayed underneath the 'Happy Birthday' banner which the children have created in 'Opportunities for IT'.

Other aspects of the English PoS covered
Speaking and listening – 2b.
Reading – 1c.

Reference to photocopiable sheet
Photocopiable page 141 may be used as a pro forma for the children's writing about their ideal birthdays.

THE GAME OF THE BOOK
To write for a purpose in response to the stimulus provided by reading a story.
†† *Whole class, working in groups or pairs.*
🕐 *At least one hour.*

Key background information
This activity involves children in thinking carefully about a book which they have read or which has been read to them. They then make a simple board game which involves movement according to throws of a die and which is also determined by instructions related to events in the story. These events appear on some of the squares. The objective is to encourage children to consider the events in the story in depth and to decide which are bad and which are good.

Preparation
Make A3 copies of photocopiable page 142 and mount on card or copy directly on to card. You will need one game board for each pair of children or one for each group. Laminate with clear self-adhesive plastic film if possible.

Resources needed
Photocopiable page 142, A3 paper, A3 card, writing and drawing materials, rulers, scissors, dice.

Show them an example of what you would like to do on your birthday, or use the photocopiable sheet, so that children can see how the events can be set out in chronological order.

Provide a word list to aid spelling and to provide ideas and ask the children to produce their own timetables for their perfect birthday. Give the children copies of photocopiable page 141 and ask them to use it to write a timetable of their ideal birthday. Encourage them to think about what they would like to eat, what they would like to do and who they would like to see on their birthdays.

Suggestion(s) for extension
Children could go on to write a story of an ideal birthday without the timetable format. They could look at other examples of timetables such as bus, train and television lists.

Suggestion(s) for support
Children could draw pictures to illustrate events in their ideal birthdays and add sentences with the help of an adult.

Assessment opportunities
Look for evidence that children are able to write chronologically and can place their ideas in the appropriate order. Note, too, interesting choices of vocabulary.

Opportunities for IT
The children could write their timetables using a word processor or simple desktop publishing package. If they use a word processor the children should be shown how to use

What to do
Show the children the game on photocopiable page 142 which is based on the story of *Jack and the Beanstalk*. The game could be played by the whole class with a large die and the class divided into two groups, or the children could play it in pairs. Show the children how the squares give information about what the players must do and that when a bad thing happens they have to move backwards, but when a good thing happens they move forwards.

When the children are familiar with the idea of the game and have played it themselves ask them to think about a story which they have read or had read to them recently. Ask them to work in pairs or small groups to make a list of good and bad things which happened in the story.

When the children have made their lists ask them to choose an equal number of good and bad things to include in their games. Then show them how to draw a board for the games, with some squares which are coloured and other squares which have writing in them. In order to avoid having children make mistakes it may be a good idea to provide squares for them to colour or write on. These may then be pasted on to the board when their accuracy has been checked. It may be that some children will be unable to make their writing small enough to fit into the squares without it becoming illegible. Ask these children to make separate 'chance' cards which can be read by players, with some squares being labelled 'chance'.

Emphasise the need for games to be well-presented and for writing to be legible and accurate. When the children have finished making their games let them try playing them to see if they need to be adjusted before letting friends try them.

Suggestion(s) for extension
Games could be made more sophisticated by adding other cards with instructions for forward or backward movement. Children could prepare sets of instructions for the games and could decorate boxes for them.

Suggestion(s) for support
Children who experience difficulties with reading and writing could work with more able pupils, but might still be responsible for copying messages written by their classmates.

A story game: Jack and the Beanstalk

Start | Jack sells cow. Mum is cross. Go back 2. | Beanstalk starts to grow. Move on 3 | Beanstalk still growing. Throw again. | Jack climbs beanstalk. Wait for a 5 or a 6 | Giant sees Jack. Go back 5 | Giant's wife hides Jack. Go on 1. | Jack takes golden goose. Go on 1. | Giant wakes up. Shake again. | Giant chases Jack. Hide and miss a turn. | Jack chops beanstalk down. Throw again. | Happily ever after

Assessment opportunities
Note the children's abilities to use the text in the book to provide them with ideas for their games. Look for evidence, when the games are played, that their designers have written with their audiences in mind.

Opportunities for IT
The children could use a word processor to write the chance cards or instructions, editing and redrafting them as the need for new rules appears. They could also use an art package to design pictures or to decorate a box for the game.

Display ideas
The children's games that they have devised themselves could be mounted on card and covered with self-adhesive plastic film and then boxed for use as a classroom resource.

Other aspects of the English PoS covered
Speaking and listening – 1a, b; 2b.
Reading – 1a, c, d; 2b, c; 3.

Reference to photocopiable sheet
Photocopiable page 142 provides a sample game based on Jack and the Beanstalk for children to play as a prelude to making their own games.

THE MIDDLE OF THE STORY

To demonstrate an increased awareness of and ability to use the characteristics of narrative writing.

†† *Whole class or group, working individually or in pairs.*

🕐 *At least one hour.*

Previous skills/knowledge needed
The children will need to have considerable experience of having stories read and told to them.

Key background information
Stories tend to have clearly defined beginnings in which the characters and situations are introduced, middles in which the story is developed, and endings in which the denouement is revealed. This activity focuses children's attention on the central part of the story and encourages them to read the introduction and ending before creating a suitable middle.

Preparation
Read stories to the children and talk with them about the beginnings, middles and endings. Make copies of photocopiable page 143, one for each child or pair.

Resources needed
A range of stories, photocopiable page 143, writing materials. Cassette player and blank cassettes for the support activity.

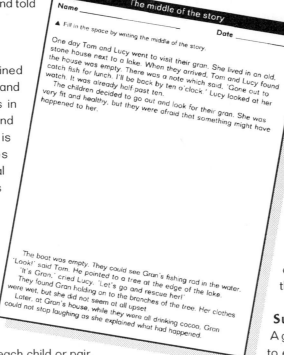

The middle of the story

Name _____ Date _____

▲ Fill in the space by writing the middle of the story.

One day Tom and Lucy went to visit their gran. She lived in an old, stone house next to a lake. When they arrived, Tom and Lucy found the house was empty. There was a note which said, 'Gone out to catch fish for lunch. I'll be back by ten o'clock.' Lucy looked at her watch. It was already half-past ten.
The children decided to go out and look for their gran. She was very fit and healthy, but they were afraid that something might have happened to her.

The boat was empty. They could see Gran's fishing rod in the water. 'Look!' said Tom. He pointed to a tree at the edge of the lake. 'It's Gran,' cried Lucy. 'Let's go and rescue her!'
They found Gran holding on to the branches of the tree. Her clothes were wet, but she did not seem at all upset.
Later, at Gran's house, while they were all drinking cocoa, Gran could not stop laughing as she explained what had happened.

What to do
Talk with the children about stories with which they are familiar and ask them to tell you about the beginnings and endings. Discuss the ways in which the characters and situations are introduced and the stories are concluded.

Talk about well-known stories such as *Sleeping Beauty* and *Little Red Riding Hood* and ask the children to describe the beginnings and endings.

Provide the children with copies of photocopiable page 143 and explain that it provides a beginning and an ending of a story. Tell the children that they need to read it carefully and then write at least three sentences to tell the middle of the story. They should think carefully about the beginning and ending and should make sure that in the middle they include the characters who are mentioned in the story. When they have finished, their writing should make it possible for the reader to enjoy a complete story.

As the children work, stop them occasionally to discuss ideas and to talk about the task and what is required. Encourage children to make their stories interesting and to think about ways in which they can engage their readers' interest.

Suggestion(s) for extension
A group of three children could be asked to each write beginnings for stories and then pass these on for middles to be written. When the middles have been written, they should be passed on once again for endings to be produced. At the end of the activity every member of the group will have a

story which has been written by three different authors. The stories could then be refined and developed through discussions between the authors.

Suggestion(s) for support
Children who experience difficulties with writing might tape-record the middle of their stories and then write these with the help of an adult. Alternatively, they could write with the help of an adult scribe.

Assessment opportunities
Look for evidence that children are able to understand story structure and can write coherently in response to the stimuli.

Opportunities for IT
The children could write the middle section of the story using a word processor. They could place their writing between the beginning and ending of the story which you have previously created as a word-processed file. The children could use a different font style, size or even colour to highlight their own part of the writing.

Display ideas
The beginnings and endings provided on the photocopiable sheet could be enlarged and displayed, together with the children's different versions of the middle section.

Other aspects of the English PoS covered
Speaking and listening – 1a.
Reading – 1a; 3.

Reference to photocopiable sheet
Photocopiable page 143 provides an example of a story with a beginning and an ending, but no middle. The children provide the middle of the story.

THE END OF THE STORY

To produce narrative writing which involves continuing and completing a story.

†† *Whole class or group, working individually or in pairs.*
🕐 *At least one hour.*

Key background information
Children's growing familiarity with stories should enable them to be able to discuss endings and suggest alternatives. This activity offers them the opportunity to look carefully at a story and at the characters who feature in it. They should be encouraged to feel that their ideas are valid and that there is no 'correct' version of the ending.

Preparation
Make copies of photocopiable page 144, one for each child

or pair. Record the story on a cassette for the support activity (optional).

Resources needed
Photocopiable page 144, scrap paper, writing materials. Cassette player and blank cassettes for support activity. Recorded cassette for support activity (optional).

What to do
Give out copies of photocopiable page 144 and read the story aloud to the children while they follow it. Talk with them about the story and about the characters in it. Ask them to imagine that they were lost in the dark. How would they feel? What would they do? What do they think that Rachel and Alex's mother should have done?

Talk with the children about the ending of the story. Ask

The end of the story

▲ Read the story and see if you can write your own ending.

It was cold and dark. Rachel and Alex were tired and hungry. It seemed like days since they had had tea but it was only five hours. If only they had stayed at home and watched television. Instead they had come with Mum on one of her walks. Mum loved to trudge through mud and up and down hills. The trouble was she was always getting lost. They were always telling her to take a map with her but she always told them that she knew the way.

This time they were really lost. No one remembered ever seeing the hills and valleys they were seeing now. The sun had set long ago and they did not have a torch. The only light came from the Moon. The trees looked like big black monsters against the moonlit sky and the only sound came from the sheep on the hillside.

'I want to go home,' said Alex.

'So do I and I don't ever want to go for a walk again!' Rachel told her mother.

Before Mum had a chance to tell them to stop grumbling they all stopped suddenly and stared.

'What is it?' asked Alex.

'I don't like it,' said Rachel.

'Come on Rachel and Alex. Let's take a closer look,' said Mum firmly.

That's the trouble with Mum, thought the children, she's never afraid of anything. The three of them began to move forward slowly in the darkness. The children gripped their mother's hands tightly and Alex closed his eyes. He only opened them when he heard Mum say, 'Oh my goodness. I've never seen anything like that before!'

▲ What had Mum, Rachel and Alex found?

▲ What do you think might happen next? Can you finish the story?

Other aspects of the English PoS covered
Speaking and listening – 1a; 2b.
Reading – 1d; 2a, b, c.

Reference to photocopiable sheet
Photocopiable page 144 provides the beginning of a story which the children continue and finish.

ARRANGING AND COMPLETING THE STORY

To interact with texts and to write endings for stories.
†† *Whole class or group, working individually or in pairs.*
🕐 *At least one hour.*

them what they think the people have seen. It is important that the children become familiar with the photocopiable sheet, which can be used as a stimulus and as an aid to spelling, since the children can refer to it for many of the words which they may need. Tell them that they are going to finish the story and that they can decide what they want to happen. Encourage them to jot down ideas for their stories before they begin and to make use of their notes when they start to write sentences.

Suggestion(s) for extension
Children could work in pairs, with each child writing the beginning of a story for the other to continue. They could complete the stories or could hand them back periodically for the other partner to develop before returning them.

Suggestion(s) for support
Children could listen to the story being read aloud on a cassette player if they find it difficult to read. Those who experience problems with writing could go on to record their own stories before being helped to write them by an adult or a writing partner.

Assessment opportunities
Look for evidence that children are able to use a narrative form and take the reader into account when writing.

Opportunities for IT
The children could use the word processor to complete their story. The start of the story could be available as a word-processed file created by you in advance. The children could highlight the part of the story they have written by using different fonts, sizes or colours.

Display ideas
The passage on photocopiable page 144 which forms the beginning of the story could be enlarged and displayed centrally, with the children's continuations displayed around it. Pictures of the central characters could be painted and cut out and added to the display.

Previous skills/knowledge needed
The children will need to be familiar with story formats and should have discussed beginnings, middles and endings of stories. The activity 'The middle of the story' might be attempted before working on this activity.

Key background information
At Key Stage 1 the National Curriculum states that children should 'be given opportunities to discuss the organisation of more complex texts' (Writing PoS). In this activity they are asked to rearrange sentences into a logical order for a story and then write a suitable ending. This will demand that children's reading skills are sufficiently advanced to enable them to read the text with understanding.

Preparation
Find a story with which the children are familiar. Make copies of photocopiable page 145, one for each child or pair.

Resources needed
Story books, photocopiable page 145, scissors, writing materials.

What to do
Talk with the children about some of the stories which they know and ask them to think of a sentence from the story and say it aloud. The sentence need not be the exact wording which appears in the book, but it should be a sentence which could appear. Ask the children to tell you whereabouts in the story the sentence might have come from. Would it be at the beginning, the middle or the end? Ask them to tell you about some of the things which have already happened in the story and some of those which have not yet occurred.

Repeat the oral activity and then use the book or books which you have chosen. Select sentences from different parts of the book and read them aloud. Ask the children whereabouts they think the sentences come from. Next, read two separate sentences from different parts of the book and ask the children which sentence appears first and invite them to explain their answers.

When the children seem familiar with the idea of identifying the parts of stories in which different sentences appear, give out the copies of photocopiable page 145. A story is provided, but its sentences are not in the right order. Explain to the children that you want them to read the sentences carefully and then arrange them in a logical sequence. Each sentence should be cut out individually. The sentences can be in a varied order, as long as the story makes sense.

When the children have arranged the sentences, ask them to think of a suitable ending for the story. Emphasise the need to include the characters already mentioned and stress the importance of making the ending interesting. Tell them that when the story ending is read, the reader should be able to find out what happened to all the different characters.

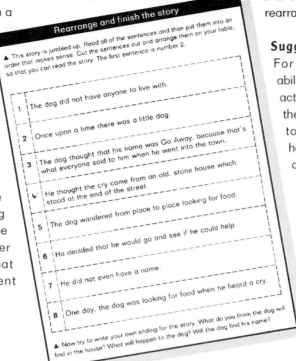

As the children write, stop them occasionally to share ideas and to discuss the sentence order which they have used. Take the opportunity to write on the board any spellings with which they may be struggling in their story endings.

Suggestion(s) for extension
Some children could go on to write their own complete stories and then cut them up for others to rearrange.

Suggestion(s) for support
For those children whose reading abilities preclude them from doing the activity, provide simpler stories and ask them to write one or two sentences to complete the stories once they have arranged them into a suitable order.

Assessment opportunities
Look for evidence that the children are able to interact with the texts and arrange them into a suitable order. In examining their story endings, look for evidence that they are able to use a narrative style and can copy spellings accurately from the text already provided.

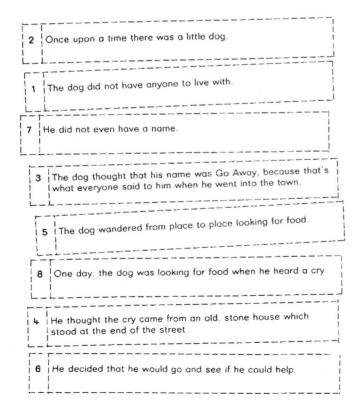

Opportunities for IT
The set of sentences used at the beginning of the activity could be typed into a word processor and the file saved. The children could then load them and reorder them into the right sequence. They will need to know how to move the text around, using either 'cut and paste' or 'drag and drop' commands. Once they have done this they can go on to write the ending of the story.

Display ideas
The completed stories could be displayed, together with examples of other jumbled stories, with sentences numbered. Children could then read these and suggest the correct order for the sentences.

Other aspects of the English PoS covered
Speaking and listening – 1a; 2a.
Reading – 1a, c; 2a, b; 3.

Reference to photocopiable sheet
Photocopiable page 145 provides a story which has been written in individual sentences placed in an incorrect order. The children are asked to arrange the sentences correctly and then complete the story.

DESCRIBE IT TO AN ALIEN

To produce descriptive writing based upon planning and note-making.

†† *Whole class or group, working individually.*

🕐 *One hour.*

Key background information

In this activity children look closely at everyday things and then describe them in writing to someone who has never heard of such things. The object is to encourage them to think carefully about the language they use and take care to describe things accurately, but without using the names of the items.

Preparation

Prepare sample descriptions of well-known items such as houses, cars, schools and trains.

Resources needed

Sample descriptions (see above), writing materials.

What to do

Begin by reading an example of a description to the children and ask them to listen carefully and try to work out what is being described. Explain that the name of the article is not used in the description but that there are lots of clues. In order to stop them from calling out as soon as they have identified the object give the children paper and pencils to write down their suggestions. The example below may be useful:

They grow from the ground and can reach great heights. Some are taller than tall buildings. Often many grow close together and people cut them down to use in making houses and furniture. They take water and food from the earth and they grow all the time, but so slowly that you would never be able to see. The parts which stick out from the central trunk are called branches and they are covered with things called leaves, although some lose these leaves in the winter.

When the children have understood the way in which the descriptions can be written tell them that they are going to attempt one of their own. Ask them to each think of something they would like to describe and make brief notes on the details of the item in question. They should then write

about it in sentences, always remembering that they are writing for someone who has never seen or heard of such a thing before. Encourage them to think of the appearance and function of the item as well as any other features, such as smell and taste, which they can think of. Explain that they should not mention the actual name of the item because their descriptions are going to be put on the wall for others to read and to guess what is being described.

If children seem to be experiencing difficulties it may be a good idea to read aloud the work of those who are succeeding or to read another example which you have prepared.

Suggestion(s) for extension

Some children could go on to produce riddles or may write more than one description.

Suggestion(s) for support

Children may require help initially with making notes. This could be done with a group in which each member writes about the same subject. Children who experience difficulty in writing in sentences could produce their writing in list form.

Assessment opportunities

Look for evidence that children are able to organise information and make appropriate vocabulary choices. Note, too, their abilities to make and work from notes.

Opportunities for IT

The children could use a word processor to write and draft their descriptions. The drafting process is important in this activity as the children refine their skills and ideas, or remove an accidental reference to the object. The final descriptions can be printed out for display in the classroom.

Display ideas

The writing can be displayed untitled for other children to read and decide what it is that each piece is describing. Pictures of the items may be displayed separately to provide clues. A large picture of an alien from another planet scratching its head in puzzlement could be painted by the children and could be a central feature of the display.

Other aspects of the English PoS covered

Speaking and listening – 1c.

LITTLE PEOPLE

To produce narrative writing which is planned and drafted in response to a stimulus.

†† *Whole class or group, working individually or in pairs.*

🕐 *One hour.*

Key background information

In this activity children have to imagine that they are very small and are asked to write stories about their adventures. The 'Borrowers' stories by Mary Norton (Puffin Classics, 1995), which have been serialised for television, are an ideal introduction to the activity. A video extract of the television serial could provide an excellent stimulus. The section of *Gulliver's Travels* by Jonathan Swift (Penguin, 1994) which takes place in Lilliput might also be used. An abridged version of this book would be most appropriate.

Preparation

Find copies of the 'Borrowers' stories and, if possible, a short extract from the television serial (if your school or LEA has an Educational Recording Agency licence), plus copies of *Gulliver's Travels*.

Resources needed

Stories about little people (see above), chalkboard, writing materials. Thesauruses at a suitable level of sophistication for the extension activity.

What to do

Introduce the activity by reading aloud extracts from the books and/or by showing part of the television serial. Ask the children what they think it would be like to be very tiny when everyone else was much bigger. Encourage them to think of both the dangers and the advantages of being small. Make a list on the board of advantages and disadvantages.

Ask the children to think of an adventure which they could have if they were very small. They can plan their stories on a sheet of paper with headings such as:

▲ What would I feel like?
▲ What I would do that I can't do now.
▲ What I would not be able to do any more.
▲ What would frighten me?
▲ What adventures could I have?
▲ How will my story end?

Ask the children to write down single words or phrases rather than sentences in their planning and tell them that when they write their stories they can make changes to their notes or add to them.

As the children write, you can read extracts from their work and talk with the whole group about the different ideas that people have had.

Suggestion(s) for extension

Children could be introduced to a simple thesaurus and be shown how to find synonyms. They could make a list of synonyms for 'small' and 'large' and could then look through their stories to find places where they could vary vocabulary to produce more interesting writing.

Suggestion(s) for support

Children could work in pairs to produce joint stories. This would allow mutual support for spelling and writing and a sharing of ideas.

Assessment opportunities

Look for evidence that children are able to plan and revise their writing and can adopt a narrative style.

Display ideas

The children's work could be made into booklets and displayed next to a model village.

Other aspects of the English PoS covered

Speaking and listening – 1a.
Reading – 1c, d.

MY FAVOURITE TOY

To produce descriptive writing based on a familiar stimulus.

†† *Whole class or group, working individually or in pairs.*
🕐 *One hour.*

Key background information
In this activity the children write about their favourite toy and describe it. You can do this activity in conjunction with, or preceding, the following activity 'The lost toy' which is linked in theme.

Preparation
Ask the children to bring their favourite toy to school. It may be a good idea to write to parents to tell them about the activity, both to reassure them that the toys will be safe at school and to explain that the children will not merely be playing with toys at school! It is advisable to restrict the children to toys which do not have lots of little pieces which could easily get lost. If possible, bring to school a favourite toy from your childhood or one of your own children's favourites.

Resources needed
Toys (see above), writing materials.

What to do
Talk with the children about your own childhood toy and explain why you liked it so much. Ask the children to talk about their favourite toys and to say what it is that they like about them. Discuss with the children the ways in which the toys work or the games which they play with them. Ask them to think of words which could be used to describe the different features of the toys and the ways in which any parts move. Make a list of the words which they offer and discuss with them how adjectives and adverbs may be used to enhance their writing.

Talk with the children about caring for their toys and tell them that some old toys can become very valuable. The presence of lots of toys in the classroom will inevitably lead to curiosity and it is important to remind children to take care of each other's property.

Tell the children that they are going to write about their favourite toy and should include a description as well as reasons why they like the toy so much. Encourage them to make use of adverbs and adjectives in their writing. It may also be a good idea to brainstorm some ideas for words which can be used to replace 'like'. These might include 'love', 'value', 'treasure', 'prize' and 'appreciate'.

As the children write, stop them occasionally to read aloud their work and to draw attention to interesting vocabulary choices and good descriptions.

Suggestion(s) for extension
A classroom museum created using toys loaned by parents and friends of the school could provide a stimulus for further work by the children. This could include looking at the history of toys and labelling exhibits. Ask the children to write letters home explaining the activity and requesting the loan of toys from parents and relations.

Suggestion(s) for support
Children who find the writing activity difficult could work with an adult helper, telling the adult about their toys and having their ideas written down before copying them out.

Assessment opportunities
Look for evidence of careful description and interesting choices of vocabulary. Can the children write in sentences? Do they use capital letters appropriately to begin sentences and for the names of toys such as teddies and dolls?

Opportunities for IT
The children could use a word processor to write the labels and descriptions for the class display of toys. They can experiment with different font styles and sizes of print to make the labels clear and easy to read.

Display ideas
A collection of toys could be displayed, with appropriate labels made by the children, and the children's writing could be put on the wall above the toys. Books about toys could also be displayed.

Other aspects of the English PoS covered
Reading – 2d.

THE LOST TOY

To produce narrative writing in cartoon form with a clearly defined beginning, middle and end.

†† *Whole class or group, working individually or in pairs.*

🕐 *At least one hour.*

Key background information

In this activity the children write a story about losing and finding a favourite toy. The initial stimulus for the work is hearing a story on a similar theme. The children are asked to illustrate their work with a series of pictures. This should serve to highlight the chronological nature of the story and enable the children who experience difficulties with writing to have a structure upon which to build their written work.

Preparation

Read *Dogger* by Shirley Hughes (Red Fox, 1993) in which a child loses his favourite toy and finds it at a jumble sale.

Resources needed

Dogger by Shirley Hughes, writing and drawing materials.

What to do

Talk with the children about their favourite toys and about how they would feel if the toys were lost. Read the story of *Dogger* to the children and ask them what they think about it. The following questions may be useful:

▲ Why did Dave not notice when he first lost Dogger?

▲ When did he realise Dogger was gone?

▲ How do you think Dave slept that night?

▲ How did he feel when he saw Dogger at the fête?

▲ Why did Bella not mind giving away her new bear?

Draw the children's attention to the need to provide a beginning, a middle and an end to the stories that *they* write.

Tell the children that now they are going to write their own stories about a lost toy, but that they must plan them carefully first. This planning may take the form of a list of ideas arranged chronologically, a series of simple pictures, or a combination of pictures and words. If the children do draw pictures it is important to emphasise at this stage that the pictures should not be too complicated but should simply show what will be happening in each part of the story. Tell the children that they will have the opportunity to draw more elaborate pictures at a later stage in the production of their story.

When the children have shown you their plans (written, drawn, or both) tell them that they must now write sentences which tell the reader more about what is happening in each picture or in each section of their list of words. Children who have not drawn pictures can do so after they have completed their writing. Those who have drawn pictures initially can spend time perfecting their drawings.

Suggestion(s) for extension

Some children might use their cartoon stories as a basis for drama work, either by acting out a play related to them, or by creating a series of tableaux which represent the pictures and reading aloud the captions which go with each.

Suggestion(s) for support

Children who experience difficulty with writing could work in pairs to draw pictures to tell their stories, working with an adult helper to produce the text. If the children tell the adult the story in each picture the adult can write the children's story for them. The children can then copy the story at a later stage.

Assessment opportunities

Note the children's abilities to plan and review their writing and to produce a narrative with a clearly defined beginning, middle and end.

Display ideas

Cartoon stories could be displayed, together with children's toys or pictures of them.

Other aspects of the English PoS covered

Speaking and listening – 1a; 2a.

Reading – 1c, d.

REPETITIVE POEMS

To write and show an appreciation of pattern in poetry.

†† *Whole class or group, working individually.*

⏱ *One hour.*

Key background information

This activity is designed as an introduction to writing poetry. The poems have a simple repetitive format which children should find easy to replicate.

Preparation

Read some examples of repetitive poems to the children. 'No' by Thomas Hood is a classic example (from *The Puffin Book of Classic Verse*, Viking, 1995), although simpler poems will need to be read too. These could include 'It's Spring, It's Spring' by Kit Wright from *A Calendar of Poems* collected by Wes Magee (Bell, Hyman 1986). Discuss with the children the poems you have selected and how the poets have used repetition for effect.

Resources needed

Examples of repetitive poems (either published poems or ones you have prepared yourself), chalkboard, writing materials.

What to do

Choose a word and write it on the left-hand side of the board several times. Add the word 'is' next to the word and ask the children to think of ways of completing the line. Encourage them to be imaginative in their choice of words and talk about whether sentences are complete. For example:

Night is dark.
Night is supper.
Night is black.
Night is cold.
Night is bedtime.
Night is lights switched off.
Night is spooky.
Night is kisses.

Other beginnings could include:

Love is...
Happiness is...
I wish...
If only...

Ask the children to choose a word of their own and to write their own poems with each line beginning in the same way. As the children write, stop them occasionally to share the ideas which they have had and to discuss spellings and imaginative use of vocabulary.

Encourage the children to experiment with language: some may even make up words. If this happens discuss the spellings of the words and talk about sound–symbol correspondence.

Suggestion(s) for extension

Children could write poems using the same format as in the main activity but with more than one verse. Each verse could use a different word.

Suggestion(s) for support

Children who find it difficult to complete the lines could be presented with a selection of words from which to choose. These might arise out of discussion with them or with the whole group.

Assessment opportunities

Look for examples of interesting and imaginative vocabulary choices.

Opportunities for IT

The children could write their poems using a word processor. They could be shown how to 'cut and paste' the starting words on to several lines to save typing them in each time. Alternatively, you could prepare a concept keyboard overlay with several starting words on it so that the children could quickly start each new line. Other words could be typed at the keyboard.

Other aspects of the English PoS covered

Speaking and listening – 3b.
Reading – 1c, b.

WEATHER POEMS

To plan and review writing and to use imaginative vocabulary.

†† *Whole class or group, working individually or in pairs.*

🕐 *One hour.*

Key background information

There are many examples of poems about the weather which might be shown to children as a stimulus for this work. The poems produced by the children might be simple adjective/noun lists or they could be more sophisticated.

Preparation

Find examples of poems about the weather. These might include the following: 'School Field in Winter' by Wes Magee in *A Fifth Poetry Book* (Oxford, 1994); 'Rain', 'The Street in Summer' and 'The Street in Winter' in *All Together Now* by Tony Bradman (Puffin, 1990); 'Who Has Seen the Wind?' by Christina Rossetti in *The Book of a Thousand Poems* (Collins, 1994).

Resources needed

Weather poems (see above), chalkboard, writing materials. Cassette recorder, blank cassettes and sound effect objects for extension activity.

What to do

Read to the children examples of poems about the weather and talk about the different ways in which the authors describe weather conditions.

Encourage them to consider the variety of adjectives and adverbs which are used and explain that we can, for instance, write about seeing 'rain falling' but can make this more interesting for the reader by describing the rain and the way in which it is falling. An example might be 'Driving rain falling heavily'.

Begin the writing activity by producing a class or group poem on the board, allowing children to offer their ideas and then writing them on the board for everyone to see. An important element of this activity is drafting. Children should be able to see that the poem which is being created can be modified and adjusted until a pleasing end product has been achieved. This idea can then be related to their own work.

Ask the children to write down their ideas for a weather poem. Encourage them to put each idea on a new line and reassure them that it is not necessary for the lines to rhyme.

Emphasise the need to draft and refine ideas and tell the children that it is all right to change or discard whole lines if they wish.

As the children work, look at their efforts and discuss adjectives and adverbs used and draw the whole group's attention to interesting descriptions. Encourage children to work towards a final, well-presented poem which can be shared with the class and with others in the school.

Suggestion(s) for extension

Children could go on to present their poems to the class or to the school in assembly, adding sound effects. 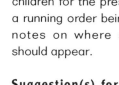 Alternatively, they could tape-record their poems with sound effects. Plans could be written by the children for the presentations, with a running order being sent out and notes on where sound effects should appear.

Suggestion(s) for support

Some children may require a more structured framework for their poems. Present them with beginnings of lines such as 'Rain is...' or 'The wind blows...' and then offer a selection of words which can be used to extend the lines.

Assessment opportunities

Look for signs that children see writing as temporary and are capable of modifying and refining their efforts to produce a final copy.

Opportunities for IT

The children could use a word processor to write and draft their poems. The children could also use authoring software to create a multimedia presentation which could include pictures drawn with an art package, sound effects recorded with a microphone connected to the computer and text written with a word processor. A title page could include different weather symbols which lead children to the pages containing their own writing.

Display ideas

Poems could be displayed, together with pictures drawn or painted by the children or photographs of different types of weather.

Other aspects of the English PoS covered

Speaking and listening – 1c.
Reading – 1d.

AUTUMN LEAVES

To produce descriptive writing using notes.

†† *Whole class or group, working individually.*

🕐 *One hour.*

Key background information
In this activity children are asked to describe different leaves. (The activity might be linked to a sorting activity in science.) This activity focuses on the use of adjectives to enhance descriptions and may be preceded by reading poetry to the children.

Preparation
Make a collection of leaves at various stages of decay. Include some which are still green and healthy and others which are brown and frangible. Look for examples which have different colours and shapes. Find some poems which describe autumn leaves, for example 'Leaves' by J.M. Westrup in *The Book of a Thousand Poems* (Collins, 1994). Prepare a word bank for children needing support work.

Resources needed
Assorted leaves, poems about leaves (see above), writing materials. Word bank for support activity.

What to do
Show the children the collection of leaves and explain to them that they are going to use their senses to describe them. Let each child choose a leaf and ask them to look at it carefully. Tell them to make notes about the shape and colour and about any other features of the leaf's appearance.

Next, ask the children to feel the leaf and to make notes about it. The children could go on to smell the leaves and listen to the sounds which are made when the leaves are crumpled up. It is not advisable to let the children taste the leaves and it may be worthwhile warning them about the dangers of tasting things which may harm them.

When the children have made notes ask them to use these to write a description of the leaves using complete sentences. As the children work, take the opportunity to share good examples with the rest of the group and discuss the ways in which the children have made use of descriptive words.

Suggestion(s) for extension
Children could describe the sounds made when walking through leaves. A group might be taken outside under supervision and allowed to walk through leaves as a stimulus for this writing.

Suggestion(s) for support
A word bank may be needed by some children to enable them to write fluently. You could include words such as 'brown', 'green', 'fragile', 'crumpled', 'broken', 'crunchy', 'ground', 'tree', 'fall', 'leaf', 'leaves', 'crackling' and 'autumn'.

Assessment opportunities
Look for imaginative vocabulary choices and interesting descriptions.

Opportunities for IT
Some children could write their leaf descriptions using a word processor or desktop publishing package. They could format their writing so that it forms the shape of a leaf. If the children start with the centre command, they can then adjust their writing, using the space bar and then the return key to separate lines. Children could illustrate their work using leaf shapes taken from clip art or drawn with an art package.

Display ideas
The children's writing could be mounted on various shades of sugar paper including yellow, brown, orange and green. This could then be double-mounted on paper cut into leaf shapes. On a table in front of the wall display, leaves could be placed and examples of poems in books could be placed on book stands.

Other aspects of the English PoS covered
Speaking and listening – 3b.
Reading – 1d.

MY IDEAL CAR

To write imaginatively after drawing.

†† *Whole class or group, working individually or in pairs.*

🕐 *One hour.*

Key background information

Here the children are asked to draw a car which they would really like and to label its parts. They will need to develop the labelling so that each item is explained. For example, 'Big wheels for going over rough ground'. A selection of model cars, including 'transformers' which can be changed from being robots, for example, into vehicles, might be a useful addition.

Preparation

Ask the children to bring model cars to school and let them show their cars to the rest of the class. Look in motoring sections of newspapers for examples of concept cars – those which manufacturers make as experiments. The BBC programme *Top Gear* often features such cars, as well as expensive or unusual cars which are manufactured and sold. Let the children see a video extract of the programme as a stimulus for this activity. Show the children the pictures of cars you have cut out of newspapers and magazines.

Resources needed

Pictures and video showing unusual cars (see above), toy cars, word bank, writing materials. Extracts from books for extension activity, for example *The Wind in the Willows* by Kenneth Grahame (Puffin, 1995), *Danny, the Champion of the World* by Roald Dahl (Puffin, 1994) and *Flossie Teacake's Fur Coat* by Hunter Davies (Armada, 1984).

What to do

Talk with the children about some of the cars which they will have met through films and stories. These might include *Chitty Chitty Bang Bang*, the Batmobile from *Batman* and 007's car in the Bond films. Talk about the special features which these cars possess and ask the children about the features which they would like to have on their cars.

Ask the children to draw their ideal cars and label the parts, especially those which are different from normal cars. When they have done this ask them to write sentences to explain the different features and their uses. Provide a bank of useful words and encourage children to suggest additional vocabulary.

As the children work, draw attention to their individual efforts and highlight interesting ideas and sentence structures.

Suggestion(s) for extension

Some children could write stories involving their ideal cars. As a stimulus for this, extracts could be read to them from *The Wind in the Willows* (Mr Toad's drive), *Danny the Champion of the World* (Danny's drive) and *Flossie Teacake's Fur Coat* (Flossie's driving lesson).

Suggestion(s) for support

Some children may need extra support from an adult for the writing. Such children could be helped as a group and supplied with suitable vocabulary based upon their ideas.

Assessment opportunities

Make a note of children's abilities to organise their work and to produce imaginative descriptions of parts of their cars.

Opportunities for IT

The children could use an art or drawing package to create their own ideal cars. They could be shown how to use the shape drawing commands to draw the round wheels, and the fill facility to add colour. The pictures could be added to word-processed writing about the car.

Display ideas

A display of model cars could be accompanied by a display of the children's writing and pictures, together with their pictures and the photographs you have collected.

Other aspects of the English PoS covered

Reading – 1d.

ACROSTICS

To use knowledge of sound–symbol correspondence and the ability to write in sentences to write acrostics.

†† *Whole class or group, working individually or in pairs.*

⏰ *One hour.*

Key background information
In this activity children are given a key word and are asked to write it vertically down the side of the page. They then have to write sentences beginning with each letter of the word which describe the word.

Preparation
Find or write examples of acrostics.

Resources needed
Examples of acrostics, dictionaries, chalkboard, writing materials.

What to do
Write a word on the board and ask the children to sound each letter. Now write the word vertically and explain that you want to write sentences beginning with each letter of the word. Ask the children for ideas and write them on the board, editing these and revising them as new suggestions come along. When the children are satisfied with the piece of writing ask them to read it individually and collectively.

Explain that the children are going to produce similar pieces of writing and that these are called 'acrostics'. It may be a good idea to have everyone working on the same word, or at least on the same theme, with a small selection of words available. However, some children may wish to use words of their own. It is important that you check that they have spelled their words correctly before they start! Talk with them about the letters in the word and their sounds and encourage those children who are able to do so to use dictionaries.

Suggestion(s) for extension
Children could go on to choose other words and make up further acrostics. They might be given a challenge such as each line having to contain at least six words.

Suggestion(s) for support
Some children may need to be given a selection of words from which they can choose most of those which go into their acrostics.

Assessment opportunities
Note the children's awareness of sound–symbol correspondence and their abilities to write in sentences. Look, too, for imaginative vocabulary choices. The activity should enable you to identify those children who require additional help with initial letter sounds.

Opportunities for IT
Children could use a word processor to write or present their acrostic. They could highlight each of the initial letters by making them larger than the rest of the sentence, using a different font, emphasis or size.

Display ideas
Acrostics could be displayed, together with appropriate pictures drawn or painted by the children.

Other aspects of the English PoS covered
Reading – 2b.

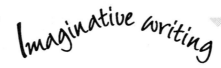

AT THE SEASIDE

To produce list writing and imaginative writing.

†† *Whole class or group, working individually or in pairs.*

🕐 *One hour.*

Previous skills/knowledge needed

The activity begins with some drama–mime work. Although not essential, it would help if children had experience of this way of working before the lesson.

Key background information

This activity is designed to lead the children from a drama activity to a written one. It may take place before or after a visit to the seaside, or just after the summer holidays when many children will have visited the coast. The initial activity is intended to offer a form of first-hand experience which should provide a stimulus for children's writing.

Preparation

Find examples of pictures of the seaside or obtain some slides or a short video extract if this is possible. Make a list of the things which might be seen at the seaside. Find a tape of seaside sounds if you can. Arrange for the use of a large room such as a hall or gym for the first part of the activity.

Resources needed

Pictures, slides or a video extract (see above), cassette player and tape of seaside sounds, chalkboard, card, writing materials. Sentence bank for support activity.

What to do

As part of a movement lesson in the hall ask the children to imagine that they are at the seaside. Tell them where the sea is and where the beach is. Ask a few at a time to go to the beach and begin to mime the things which they would do. The children may be told, at first, what they are to do on the beach, for example paddling, making sandcastles, playing with a bat and ball, looking in rock pools, sunbathing, having a picnic, digging in the sand or getting ready to go for a swim. It may add authenticity if a tape of the seaside can be played during the activity.

When the children return to the classroom ask them to write down all the things which they 'saw' at the seaside. Encourage them to add describing words and to build the writing into a descriptive passage. Stop the children regularly to talk about the words which they are using and to help with spelling by writing some words on the board or on cards which could be placed on a display based on a seaside theme (see 'Display ideas').

At this stage, a video extract, some slides or some photographs of the seaside will help the children to think of different features of a visit.

Ask the children to write sentences about different aspects of the seaside, encouraging them to make use of nouns and adjectives which describe what they would be able to see and hear. The sentences can later be combined to create a piece of prose or writing set out in poetic form.

Suggestion(s) for extension

Children could focus on a single aspect of the seaside and could write about this. They might concentrate on the sound of the sea, sea shells, sand, games on the beach, seagulls, food, pebbles and so on.

Suggestion(s) for support

For some children a sheet of unfinished sentences to complete might be useful for support. These could be set out as follows:

At the seaside I like to play...
On the beach I like to...
At the seaside I can hear...
I like to eat _____ at the seaside.

Assessment opportunities

Note the children's abilities to make interesting vocabulary choices and to write in sentences.

Opportunities for IT

The children could use a word processor to write their list and draft it into full prose. A concept keyboard with starting phrases could also be used for some children.

Display ideas

Writing could be displayed against a background frieze of the seaside produced by the children. Seagulls could be drawn and painted and could be hung from the ceiling in front of the display. Sea shells, sand and pebbles could be placed on a table in front of the frieze. Given the abrasive effect of sand on floors, it may be a good idea to place the sand on trays with lips, or to put a strip of card slightly elevated from the table underneath the sand.

Other aspects of the English PoS covered

Speaking and listening – 1d.

PICTURE STORIES

To produce chronological story writing in response to a stimulus.

☨☨ *Whole class or group, working individually or in pairs.*

🕐 *One hour.*

Key background information

In this activity the children are presented with a story in pictures and are asked to write a sentence to describe what is happening in each picture.

Preparation

Make copies of photocopiable pages 146 and 147 – one copy of both sheets for each child or pair.

Resources needed

Photocopiable pages 146 and 147, chalkboard, writing materials. Comics for extension activity.

What to do

Give the children copies of the first story on photocopiable page 146 and ask them to tell you what is happening in each picture. Show them how their ideas may be written in sentences to provide a written description of the picture story. Write sentences on the board which the children can copy on to their sheet, writing underneath the pictures.

Now give out copies of the second picture story on photocopiable page 147 and ask the children to tell you what is happening in it. Write some key words on the board, but do not write sentences for the children. Ask

the children to write their own sentences to describe what is happening in the story (one sentence for each picture). Emphasise the need to begin sentences with capital letters and end them with full stops. Talk with them about making their stories interesting and draw attention, as they write, to examples of adjectives and adverbs which make descriptions more interesting.

Suggestion(s) for extension

Some children could go on to produce their own stories in words and pictures. A starting point could be a single picture chosen from a comic, with the children being asked to add their own pictures and then write sentences describing them.

Suggestion(s) for support

Some children may need the support of a partner or an adult who can help them to write down their ideas. The ideas could be written as partially completed sentences and children could be asked to finish these. This could enable the adult to discuss the concept of a sentence with the children and to let them see an experienced writer at work.

Assessment opportunities
Note the children's abilities to relate their writing to the pictures and their abilities to use a narrative style in their chronological writing.

Display ideas
Pictures and writing could be displayed, together with examples from published works such as comics and annuals. The children might put their work together, if they have created their own picture stories, to make comics which could be photocopied, coloured and distributed.

Other aspects of the English PoS covered
Speaking and listening – 1a.

Reference to photocopiable sheets
Photocopiable pages 146 and 147 provide two picture stories, one to be discussed at the beginning of the lesson before being completed and the other for children to work on independently.

SOUND POETRY

To make choices about vocabulary and to produce collaborative writing.
†† *Children working in pairs.*
🕐 *Approximately one hour.*

Previous skills/knowledge needed
Children will need to be familiar with the structure and rhythm of poems.

Key background information
As children's writing becomes more sophisticated, they will make greater use of adjectives and adverbs. This activity provides a stimulus for them to describe the sounds they hear in different parts of the school. They will need to be able to use a simple portable cassette recorder and should be able to work co-operatively with other children.

Preparation
Prepare a word bank which lists a vocabulary for describing sounds. Find light, portable cassette players which can be operated easily by children.

Resources needed
Cassette players and blank cassettes, word bank (see above), chalkboard, writing materials.

What to do
Tell the children that they are going to write a 'school sounds' poem for assembly or for a parents' evening, to help people who are not usually in the school when the children are there to understand more about the school. Talk with the children about sounds and the words which may be used to describe them. Play a recording of some sounds and ask the children to try to identify them and to describe the noises. Write their suggestions on the board to build up a word bank for later writing.

Provide pairs of children with a cassette player and ask them to visit different parts of the school and record two minutes of sounds. It is important to define for them the areas which they may visit and to make sure that colleagues are aware of what the children are doing. The children might, with approval, visit the kitchens, the office, the gymnasium or hall, different classrooms, the school library, the playground and the dining hall.

When the children have compiled their tape of sounds, work with them to brainstorm ideas for each of the two-minute sections. The children may do this independently, but some may benefit from having a more experienced writer to note their ideas.

Ask the children to work together to write a four-line poem to describe the sounds they heard in one area. It is not necessary that the poem should rhyme. The format could

Suggestion(s) for support

Where composition is difficult because of poor writing skills, children could record their poem on a cassette player which could be transcribed at a later stage with the assistance of an adult helper.

Assessment opportunities

Note children's use of imaginative vocabulary and their abilities to respond to constructive criticism when revising their work.

Opportunities for IT

The children could use authoring software to create a multimedia sound poem which could include the sounds they have recorded along with the descriptions written. It could even include pictures of the source of the sound.

Other aspects of the English PoS covered

Speaking and listening – 1a.
Reading – 2a.

THE HOLE IN THE FENCE

To develop the ability to write imaginatively and with confidence, fluency and accuracy in response to a stimulus.

†† *Whole class or group, working individually.*

⏲ *At least one hour.*

---

be based upon the first word of each line being descriptive of the noise, followed by words which identify it in more detail. For example:

> Chattering children eating lunch.
> Crunching of apples and crisps.
> Crashing of cutlery in trays.
> Sloshing of water into jugs.
>
> Scraping of pens on paper.
> Screeching of chalk on the board.
> Whispering of children at tables.
> Grumbling of teacher at his desk.

When the children have written a verse for one part of the school, ask them to read it aloud to the class who may try to identify the part of the school which they have written about. Encourage constructive criticism and redrafting until the piece is ready for presentation to an audience.

Children may go on to write a verse for each section of their tape recording.

Suggestion(s) for extension

Children could work independently, out of school hours, to write a poem for a place familiar to their classmates. This might be the park, the street, the supermarket. They should not tell others where their poem is set, but should read it to them so that they can guess.

Key background information

In this activity children are presented with the beginning of a story about a child who moves to a new house and becomes curious about what might be on the other side of the fence at the bottom of the garden. After reading the story, or having it read to them, the children are asked to continue the tale and write about the child's adventures.

Just as C.S. Lewis cautions children about climbing into wardrobes in *The Lion, the Witch and the Wardrobe* (HarperCollins, 1994), it may be a good idea to warn children about the dangers of going into places where they may meet dangers.

This activity should allow children the opportunity to write at length and should enable you to assess a number of features of their writing.

Preparation

Make copies of photocopiable page 148, one for each child.

Resources needed

Photocopiable page 148, chalkboard, writing materials.

What to do

Use photocopiable page 148 to tell the children the beginning of the story about the child who finds a hole in a fence. Give out copies of the story on the photocopiable sheet and ask the children to talk about what the child might find on the other side of the fence. Let them share their ideas with the whole group and write on the board any words which are likely to be needed by many children in the class.

Ask the children to make notes on how they think the story could continue and then ask them to use their notes to help them to write the rest of the story. Encourage them to use adjectives and adverbs to make their writing more interesting (you could provide some suitable words on the board if necessary) and stop them occasionally to read aloud examples of good work.

Suggestion(s) for extension

The activity might be developed through drama work, with children acting out their stories in mime or with a commentary.

Suggestion(s) for support

Some children might tell their stories in cartoon form with a sentence for each picture. Children who experience difficulty

with spellings might be encouraged to 'have a go' at words which they are unsure of. This will enable you to make judgements about the children's knowledge of sound–symbol correspondence.

Assessment opportunities

Look for imaginative use of vocabulary and well-structured stories with well-organised text. Note the extent to which children are able to work independently, and look for signs that they are forming letters correctly and understand the directional nature of writing.

Display ideas

Children's stories could be mounted on the wall and then a large paper fence could be displayed about 30cm in front of the work, with holes through which the stories can be read.

Other aspects of the English PoS covered

Speaking and listening – 1a.
Reading – 1d.

Reference to photocopiable sheet

Photocopiable page 148 provides the beginning of a story about a child finding a hole in a fence. The children are asked to think about what happens next and then to try to finish the story.

The hole in the fence

Name _____ Date _____

I was walking around the garden of our new house on the day after we moved in when I noticed that there was a very tall wooden fence at the end of the garden. I did not remember seeing the fence before and I became very curious about what might be behind it.

The wood was old and dark brown and the fence was much too high for me to see over it. Even if someone had lifted me up I would not have been able to see what was on the other side.

I walked up and down the garden next to the fence and I tried to imagine what might be on the other side. It was quiet and the only sounds came from birds singing and distant traffic. The sun shone warmly and the sky was clear and blue. I really wanted to know what was on the other side of the fence. Perhaps there would be children I could play with or a dog I could make friends with. There could be trees to climb or a field to play in.

I had just decided that I would never be able to find out what was on the other side of the fence when I noticed a small gap right in the middle. I looked at it carefully. If I tried hard I thought I might be able to squeeze through the hole and then I would be able to explore.

▲ What do you think happens next? Can you finish the story? Use the back of this sheet.

Non-fiction writing

This chapter provides activities which should extend the range and scope of children's writing. The influence of the National Writing Project, and the introduction of the National Curriculum, seem to have broadened the writing experiences of young children. The main diet of story writing has been replaced by an emphasis upon diversity of genres. This chapter includes a variety of writing activities which should expand children's knowledge of, and ability to use, features of non-fiction writing.

Much of the writing which children see around them in shops and streets takes the form of posters and advertisements. Activities within this section encourage children to consider ways of presenting their writing effectively, for real audiences, in the way that advertisers do. They will be involved in making signs, invitations and greetings cards, as well as in making lists, recording observations and writing letters. The activities are designed to mirror those in which more experienced writers are involved.

While the majority of the activities may be completed within one writing session, some of them require children to continue their writing over an extended period. Once again, this is a feature of the writing of more sophisticated writers. By involving children in such 'real' writing, and by providing them with real audiences for their work, it is hoped that they will see writing as a purposeful and worthwhile activity and one which may constantly be developed and improved upon.

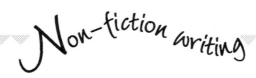
 SAY NO TO STRANGERS

To convey a message in a visual form by producing well-presented posters.

†† *Whole class or group, working individually or in pairs.*

🕐 *One hour.*

Key background information
This activity is designed not only to demonstrate the importance of children being wary of strangers, but also to encourage the production of posters and consideration of the devices which may be used to increase their impact upon the reader. The activity is strongly based within moral and social education and this element should be emphasised through discussions with the children about the dangers of going with strangers. In producing posters for others to read it is hoped that the children will think carefully about potential dangers, as well as about ways in which they can present their posters.

Preparation
Provide the children with a range of examples of posters and advertisements. You will also need to provide posters which deal with children protecting themselves against people whom they do not know. Talk with the children about the ways in which posters are designed to create the maximum impact.

Resources needed
Samples of 'Say No to strangers' posters and/or other posters and advertisements, scrap paper, A3 paper, writing and drawing materials. 'Stranger danger' pamphlets for extension activity.

What to do
Talk with the children at length about strangers and how they should respond to them. Ask them to tell each other what a stranger is and whom they should and should not trust.

Ask them to design a poster for younger children who 'might not be as sensible as they are' to tell them about the message 'Never go with strangers' or 'Say No to strangers'. Talk to them about the importance of keeping the message simple but clear and about the value of careful and attractive presentation. Published examples may provide ideas.

Provide children with a bank of words which might prove useful such as 'danger', 'stranger', 'careful', 'refuse' and 'never'.

Encourage the children to plan their posters on scrap paper before committing their ideas to A3 good quality paper. Talk with them about layout and the use of various print sizes to highlight messages. Before they produce their final versions encourage them to check spellings carefully.

Suggestion(s) for extension
Children could be shown examples of pamphlets and brochures about 'stranger danger' and could be asked to design their own, using features of presentation which they have learned through the main activity.

Suggestion(s) for support
Some children may need help with setting work out. A common problem is that children do not allow themselves sufficient room to fit in complete words. Encourage them to write very faintly at first so that they ensure that they will be able to fit their writing on to the paper.

Assessment opportunities
Note the children's abilities to present work clearly, neatly and attractively in order to communicate meaning effectively. Look for evidence that the children have understood the messages which the posters were designed to convey.

Opportunities for IT
The children could use an art or drawing package to produce their poster. They could add text, selecting appropriate fonts, and resize them to fit the available space. They could then add suitable illustrations which they could draw themselves, take from collections of clip art or scan from their own line drawings. Similar results could be obtained using a desktop publishing package or word processor.

Older or more able children could go on to use a simple desktop publishing package to write a pamphlet. A useful format is an A4 sheet folded into six vertical columns in the form of a 'three-fold'. This gives six panels of information spread over both sides of the paper.

Display ideas
Posters could be displayed around the school and might be featured in an assembly in which the children talk about their work and the dangers of going with strangers.

Other aspects of the English PoS covered
Speaking and listening – 1b.

WHAT CAN I DO WITH MY HANDS?

To record ideas in a diagrammatic form.

†† *Whole class or group, working individually or in pairs.*

🕐 *One hour.*

Key background information

In this activity children are asked to consider all the different things which they can do with their hands. The work might be linked to a topic on 'Ourselves'. You may wish to avoid this activity if there are manually disabled children in the class. This activity offers a chance to revisit chart making, which may already have been experienced in the 'Happy charts' work on page 50. It is important that children see that this method of presentation may be used for a range of writing activities.

Preparation

Provide a range of equipment which requires manual dexterity to operate, for example needle and thread, balls, pencils, bats.

Resources needed

Equipment which can be manipulated with the hands (see above), writing materials.

What to do

Show the children the equipment which you have provided and invite some to take turns to show how different items work. Ask the children to tell you what we need to be able to do to use the items, and elicit from them that all of them require us to use our hands.

Talk with the children about all of the things which we use our hands for and ask them how they think they would manage if they were not lucky enough to have hands. Discuss left- and right-handedness and reassure them that there is nothing wrong with being left-handed. Some children may have experienced a broken arm or finger and may have had to cope without the use of one hand for a time. Ask them to talk about the things which they found difficult.

Ask the children to make a chart to show some of the different uses for our hands. This could take the form of a circle drawn in the middle of the page with the word 'hands', or the clause 'We use our hands to...', written inside it. The children then draw lines from the circle to a space near to the edge of the paper and write a different use for hands at the end of each line.

Suggestion(s) for extension

Children could use dictionaries to make a collection of words which relate to hands. They could go on to write sentences to include the words in order to show their meaning. These might include 'handbag', 'handcuff', 'handkerchief', 'handle', 'handshake' and 'handwriting'.

Suggestion(s) for support

Some children might attempt the chart but use pictures and single words to define the uses of hands.

Assessment opportunities

Note the children's abilities to present their work as a diagram.

Display ideas

A display of the children's writing could be mounted on the wall with a border round the edge composed of hands which the children have produced by drawing round each other's hands, and then colouring and cutting out the resulting pictures.

Other aspects of the English PoS covered

Speaking and listening – 1c.

CHRISTMAS STOCKINGS

To copy words accurately and to label clearly.

†† *Whole class or group, working individually.*

🕐 *One hour.*

Key background information

In this activity children make a paper Christmas stocking and draw or cut out pictures of presents which are then stuck on to the stocking and labelled. The activity is designed to develop vocabulary, copying skills and to encourage careful presentation.

Preparation

Find catalogues which feature toys and other items which would be suitable as Christmas gifts. Make copies of photocopiable page 149 (enlarged, if necessary) and cut out a stocking for each child who is doing the activity. Make a Christmas stocking by cutting out and completing the photocopiable sheet yourself to provide a good visual aid and stimulus.

Resources needed

Catalogues, photocopiable page 149, glue, scissors. Vocabulary list for extension activity.

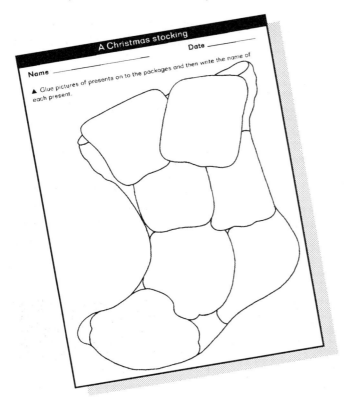

What to do

Explain to the children that they are going to make a Christmas stocking and choose presents to go with it. Give out the stockings, cut out from copies of photocopiable page 149. Tell the children that the stocking could be for a friend or a member of their family. Talk with them about the kinds of presents which the recipient might like to receive and encourage the children to look in the catalogues to find pictures.

Show the children how to cut out the pictures and how to use glue carefully to stick them on to the stocking. Draw their attention to the descriptions of the gifts in the catalogues and tell them that they need to write underneath their pictures the name of each item which they have put on their stocking.

As the children work, show examples of accurate copying of words and neat presentation to the rest of the group.

Suggestion(s) for extension

Children could write about opening their own presents. They could be encouraged to describe their feelings as they discovered what was in their stockings. A vocabulary list may be provided including words such as 'unwrapped', 'thrilled', 'delighted', 'surprised' and 'grateful'.

Suggestion(s) for support

Some children may need help to find the names of gifts in the catalogues. Show them how the letters or numbers on the pictures correspond to those next to the descriptions and work alongside them to help them to read the necessary words.

Assessment opportunities

Note the children's abilities to write from left to right and to form letters correctly.

Display ideas

Stockings could be displayed on the wall or, if the children paste pictures and write words on both sides of the stockings, they could be hung from the ceiling or from a washing-line.

Other aspects of the English PoS covered

Reading – 2d.

Reference to photocopiable sheet

Photocopiable page 149 provides a template for a Christmas stocking which is copied and cut out, then decorated with pictures of presents, each one being labelled.

I WENT ON MY HOLIDAY...

To make simple notes as aide-mémoires.
†† *Whole class or group.*
🕐 *30 minutes.*

Key background information

This activity is based upon the traditional parlour game in which each participant takes a turn to say a sentence beginning 'I went on my holiday and I took with me...' The activity is developed so that children are allowed to make notes to help them to remember all the items.

Preparation
Make sure that the children are familiar with the game 'I went on my holiday'. Copy photocopiable page 150, one copy for each child.

Resources needed
Photocopiable page 150, writing materials.

What to do
Begin the activity by playing 'I went on my holiday' orally. Each time a new person has a turn, he or she has to say all the previous items before adding a new one. As children fail to remember items, they are eliminated from the game. As the children begin to find it difficult to remember items in the growing list, ask them what would help them to remember. If they do not suggest writing notes, ask them if they think that this would be a good idea. Provide them with copies of photocopiable page 150 and tell them that they can make notes to help them to remember items. Encourage them to use experimental or temporary spellings when they do not know how to write a word and explain that you will show them the correct spellings at the end of the game. The most important thing at this stage is to play the game and remember as many items as possible.

It may be a good idea to tell the children that no one will look at their notes unless invited to do so, so they are free to try out spellings without fear of being embarrassed if they make mistakes.

Suggestion(s) for extension
Children could be encouraged to make use of note-taking in other aspects of their work. For example, they could make notes when finding out about a topic from books or when watching an educational television programme.

Suggestion(s) for support
Children who experience difficulty in making notes could be encouraged to draw simple sketches when unable to write words.

Assessment opportunities
Look for examples of note-making and children's abilities to relate their notes to the game.

Other aspects of the English PoS covered
Speaking and listening – 1c.
Reading – 1a.

Reference to photocopiable sheet
The children can write in the spaces provided on each 'suitcase' on photocopiable page 150 to help them to remember as many items as possible when playing the game 'I went on my holiday'.

SIGNS FOR THE SCHOOL/ CLASSROOM

To present writing carefully for an audience.
†† *Whole class or group, working individually or in pairs.*
🕐 *One hour.*

Key background information
This activity is designed to be undertaken in conjunction with a study of environmental print. It is intended to develop children's awareness of print around the school and to allow them to create their own signs.

Preparation
Make a collection of signs or photographs of signs and arrange to take the children for a literacy walk in which they will see lots of signs.

Resources needed
Selection of signs (these can be pictures or photographs of signs), card, chalkboard, writing and drawing materials.

What to do

Show the children examples of signs which can be found both inside and outside the school. If possible, take the children on a walk in which they will be able to see examples of different kinds of signs. Show the children pictures of signs and discuss with them why we need so many signs. Discuss the ways in which some signs convey meaning without words while other signs need to be written.

Ask the children what sort of signs could be useful in the classroom and school. These might include a 'Do not disturb' notice for silent reading sessions or story time, guidance on which side of the corridor to walk along, labels for apparatus, or general information. Write some key words on the board so that the children will be able to use them when they make their own signs.

Before asking the children to make their own signs, talk with them about the importance of careful and clear presentation and the need to make writing large enough to be read easily when people are moving. Stress the importance of the children planning their signs carefully and writing faintly at first, so that they can ensure that all letters are evenly sized and will fit on the card or paper. Talk about the height at which signs should be placed so that people can read them easily.

Suggestion(s) for extension

A class notice-board could be developed, with children putting up their own notices and adverts.

Suggestion(s) for support

Some children may need to concentrate on the pictorial aspects of signs, with support for writing being given by an adult helper.

Assessment opportunities

Note accuracy of spelling and the children's abilities to present their writing legibly and so that meaning is effectively communicated.

Opportunities for IT

The children could be given the opportunity to create their signs using a word processor or drawing package. They can select appropriate fonts, make them large enough to read and even add illustrations to make the signs more interesting.

Display ideas

Signs could be displayed around the school or the classroom so that the children see them as functional.

Other aspects of the English PoS covered

Speaking and listening – 3b.
Reading – 1b, c.

SHOPPING LISTS

To make accurate use of simple words and phrases.

†† *Whole class or group, working individually or in pairs.*

🕐 *One hour.*

Key background information

This activity forms part of a series of activities related to the theme of shopping (those on pages 26–27 and 91–92). Children are encouraged to look closely at the labelled items in a class shop and produce a shopping list. The activity can easily be linked to mathematical work in the school shop with each item having a price and children being given play money to buy the goods on their lists.

Preparation

Create a class shop using empty food packets and containers. (An ordinary table can be used for the counter.) Label items and provide price lists and price labels.

Resources needed

Class shop (see above), writing materials. Lists of items for support activity.

What to do

Talk with the children about shopping lists and ask if their parents make these. Ask them why people make lists and tell them that they are going to make their own shopping lists for visiting the class shop.

Talk with them about the different items in the class shop and draw their attention to labels and to names on packaging. Tell them that they can look carefully at the items in the shop and decide which they would like to buy and then make a shopping list. Encourage them to look closely at the ways in which words are spelled.

The styles of printing on some products may be unfamiliar to the children so it may be worth talking with them about the different ways in which letters can be written.

Suggestion(s) for extension
Children could make shopping lists for visits to real shops and you could take a small group shopping with parents' permission.

Suggestion(s) for support
Provide lists of items, with a space next to each item, so that children can look through the list with you and tick those things which they wish to include on their own lists. When you are confident that they are able to read the words, ask the children to copy them on to their own lists.

Assessment opportunities
Look for signs that children are able to copy words accurately and form letters carefully and correctly.

Display ideas
The children's shopping lists could be displayed around the labelled goods in the class shop.

Other aspects of the English PoS covered
Reading – 2b.

SHOP POSTERS

To write for an audience in a concise and eye-catching way.

†† *Whole class or group, working individually or in pairs.*
🕐 *One hour.*

Previous skills/knowledge needed
This activity can be used as a follow-up to the 'Shopping lists' activity. Children should have some knowledge of the different items which the class shop stocks.

Key background information
In this activity children devise posters and labels which are designed to encourage 'shoppers' to buy products.

Preparation
Make a collection of posters from shops to show to the children. Bring in, or ask the children to obtain, some empty food packages and containers.

Resources needed
Posters advertising goods, empty packages (see above), scrap paper, A3 paper, writing and drawing materials. List of key words for support activity.

What to do
Talk with the children about a selection of packages and posters and advertisements for different products. Discuss with them the ways in which packaging and advertisements are used to encourage us to buy the products. Talk about the ways in which the size of print varies so that our attention is drawn to certain parts of the posters. Discuss the use of colour and of pictures, and talk about the words which are used to describe products. Advertisements for supermarkets tend to include lots of references to prices. Talk with the children about these. They may find it interesting that so many items are priced at 99p rather than £1.

Explain to them that they are going to make posters advertising different products for their class shop. Ask each child to choose a particular item and then to think carefully about what he or she likes about the product. Encourage the children to think of interesting adjectives to describe it. Ask them to look carefully at the packages and to make sure that they copy words down accurately. Encourage them to plan their posters and to look at the examples which you have provided for ideas.

Suggestion(s) for extension
Children could go on to design their own packaging and could cover boxes and other containers with their own work. They could make up their own names for products.

Suggestion(s) for support

Some children may need to work with more able partners to produce posters, but they should be encouraged to join in the writing activity and to take turns at writing. A list of key words could be provided to help children with spellings. These might include names of products as well as adjectives such as 'new', 'fresh', 'delicious', 'improved', 'juicy' and 'tasty'.

Assessment opportunities

Look for signs that children are able to copy words accurately and present their work attractively using both capital and lower-case letters.

Opportunities for IT

Some children could use an art or drawing package to produce their poster. They could add text, select appropriate fonts and re-size them to fit into the space. They could then add suitable illustrations which they have drawn themselves or scanned from actual labels or their own line drawings.

Display ideas

Posters may be displayed in and around the class shop. If possible a local shopkeeper could be involved in judging a poster competition, or copies of posters might be sent to public relations departments of manufacturers for their responses.

Other aspects of the English PoS covered

Reading – 2b.
Speaking and listening – 1a; 2b.

A LETTER FROM A VISITOR

To use a range of reading and writing skills in an ongoing activity and to be aware of the communicative nature of writing.

†† *Whole class or group, working collectively, then individually or in pairs.*

⏱ *One hour initially, but the activity may be expanded considerably over a period of weeks.*

Previous skills/knowledge needed

Children will need to have some idea about letters and their functions.

Key background information

This activity is designed to initiate a series of written activities in which the children correspond with a 'visitor' to the classroom. The visitor leaves a letter after each visit and the children respond either individually or as a class.

Preparation

Find a doll, teddy bear or another suitable 'visitor'. Make an enlarged copy of photocopiable page 151, mount it on card (or photocopy on to card) and laminate it with self-adhesive plastic film.

Resources needed

Photocopiable page 151, doll or teddy bear (see above), A3 paper, A3 card, chalkboard, writing materials. List of questions for support activity.

What to do

Before the children arrive at school, place a teddy bear or doll in a prominent position in the classroom. When the children ask about it, tell them that you do not know where it came from or what it is called. Ask them to try to think of a name for it. On the following day the teddy or doll should disappear. A letter should be left in its place – use or adapt the enlarged copy of photocopiable page 151. The letter provides information and asks questions. It should be read aloud with the children so that they fully understand its contents.

Tell the children that when one receives a letter, it is polite to reply. Discuss with the children the things which they would like to include in a reply. Make notes at the side of the board so that they can see the letter being planned. The children may be able to help with this.

Talk with the children about how they would like the letter to begin and write the first sentence on the board. As the letter is being written, talk with the children about the spellings and about your use of capital letters and full stops.

When the letter is finished some children may be able to use the ideas to write their own letters. Others may copy the letter and then add their own ideas.

The visitor should respond to the class letter, giving more information and asking the children some different questions. Some children might write individual responses while others may contribute to a whole class letter.

The visitor's letters could provide details of where he or she has been. Postcards could be 'sent' to the children. Encourage them to look on the back of the postcards to see where they have come from and perhaps find out the locations of places on maps. Souvenirs could be left by the visitor.

The correspondence may continue over a number of weeks and may be revived after a break of several weeks if the children become inquisitive about the whereabouts of the visitor.

Suggestion(s) for extension

As the correspondence develops the children should be encouraged to develop greater independence in their letter writing and may be asked to write letters unaided. The children could write stories about the things which they think that their visitor does when he or she is away. Cards could be made for the visitor's birthday and for Christmas.

Suggestion(s) for support

Some children may need to have a structure for their responses. They might simply write answers next to a list of questions from the visitor and may write one or two questions with help from an adult or from a writing partner.

Assessment opportunities

Look for evidence that children appreciate that writing is a means of communication. Note their abilities to write questions and answers.

Opportunities for IT

As the activity progresses the children could take it in turns to write their letter using a word processor. They can be shown how to use the right justify command to position the address, or how to centre 'Yours sincerely'. The letters can be printed out and used as part of the class display.

Display ideas

Letters from the visitor should be written in large print and should be displayed so that children can discuss them. Postcards and greetings cards may be displayed too, together with maps to show where they have come from.

Other aspects of the English PoS covered

Speaking and listening – 1a; 3b.
Reading – 1c.

Reference to photocopiable sheet

Photocopiable page 151 provides a letter from a visitor which the children can respond to in writing.

LABELLING A BICYCLE

To label and copy words accurately.
†† *Whole class or group, working individually or in pairs.*
⏲ *One hour.*

Key background information

In this activity the children will produce labels for the parts of a bicycle. Labelling is an important aspect of both early and more developed writing. It enables children to see how writing can be related to real situations and reinforces spelling and presentational skills. Children's interest may be aroused by listening to the story *Mrs Armitage on Wheels* by Quentin

Blake (Picture Lions Series, 1990). The story tells of Mrs Armitage's many attempts to add accessories to her bicycle and the ultimate disaster which results.

Preparation

Bring a bicycle to school, if possible, and position it in a prominent but safe and secure place in the classroom. Photocopy the picture of a bicycle on photocopiable page 152. You will need one copy for each child or pair. Find colourful pictures of bicycles. These are available in manufacturers' brochures from cycle shops and in mail-order magazines. Find a copy of *Mrs Armitage on Wheels* by Quentin Blake.

Resources needed

Bicycle (optional), pictures of bicycles (see above), *Mrs Armitage on Wheels* by Quentin Blake, photocopiable page 152, chalkboard, card, writing and drawing materials, glue, Blu-Tack.

What to do

Read the story of Mrs Armitage and show the children the pictures of bicycles. Discuss the different accessories which may be added to a bicycle.

If you have been able to bring a bicycle into school, show it to the children and talk with them about its different parts. Some children will be able to ride a two-wheeled bicycle but others may only be able to do so with the aid of stabilisers. (A little research in advance may be worthwhile if the children are to be presented with the sort of machine with which they are familiar.) Ask the children what the different parts of the bicycle are called and make a list on the board. (Refer to photocopiable page 152 so that the list on the board is consistent with the names of parts given on the sheet.) Some items could be labelled by sticking word cards to the bicycle with Blu-Tack. Give out the copies of photocopiable page 152 and ask the children to use the list of words at the top of the sheet to help them to label the bicycle.

Refer constantly to your list of words on the board and discuss the spellings of the words used. Encourage the children to 'look–cover–write–check' when writing the words (Margaret Peters, 1985). Ask the children to colour the bicycle on the photocopiable sheet using any colours which they wish to use. When they label the bicycle ask them to write the name of each part in the boxes provided. The colours can be written underneath the boxes.

Suggestion(s) for extension

Some children could go on to draw their own bicycles at home. They could label their pictures and perhaps write a sentence describing the function of each part. If you have the opportunity, you could bring in an unusual bicycle, such as a tandem (or even a penny farthing borrowed from a museum!), for the children to draw, label and write about, noting special features.

Suggestion(s) for support

Some children could be given words on individual pieces of card. These may be used to label the bicycle by sticking them in the appropriate places on the photocopiable sheet before tracing over the words with a felt-tipped pen.

Assessment opportunities

Look for evidence that children are able to copy words accurately and are able to relate print to pictures. For those children who go on to write sentences, look for appropriate vocabulary choices and the use of full stops and capital letters.

Opportunities for IT

If you have a bicycle on display, each child could use the word processor to make a label to attach to different parts of the bicycle. The children could use various fonts and sizes to make the labels more interesting, perhaps adding a border to each label.

Display ideas

A display of the completed worksheets could be accompanied by pictures of different bicycles.

Other aspects of the English PoS covered

Speaking and listening – 1a, c; 3b.
Reading – 2b, d.

Reference to photocopiable sheet

Photocopiable page 152 provides a picture of a bicycle with spaces for labelling and a list of names of parts of the bicycle. The children can use the list as a word bank from which to label the bicycle correctly.

LOST AND FOUND

To present accurate descriptive writing for an audience.

†† *Whole class or group, working individually or in pairs.*

🕐 *One hour.*

Key background information

In this activity the children will write a description of a bicycle which has been found so that the owner might be able to identify it. The emphasis in the writing will be on accurate descriptions. This activity may be used as a creative follow-up to 'Labelling a bicycle' on page 93.

Preparation

Find examples of lost and found notices from local newspapers. There are some examples on photocopiable page 153. Real-life advertisements will add verisimilitude to the activity. Make copies of photocopiable page 153, one for each child or pair.

Resources needed

Lost and found advertisements (see above), photocopiable page 153, chalkboard, writing materials.

What to do

Show the children the lost and found notices and give out copies of photocopiable page 153. Tell the children that you would like them to imagine that a missing bicycle has been found and ask them what information they would need to provide if the owner were to be able to identify the bicycle from its description. Write some of their ideas on the board and then ask them to write their own 'found' notices. If bicycles are brought to school by older children, it may be possible to arrange to use one of them for the activity. The children could then be provided with a real audience for their writing by taking descriptions to the children from the older class and asking them if they fitted their bicycles.

Tell the children that their descriptions should not be too long because people may be put off reading them, but they should provide sufficient detail for the owner to be able to identify his or her bicycle.

Encourage the children to look for features of the bicycle which might be unique to it and to use adjectives to describe the different aspects of the bicycle, for example colour of frame, type of handlebars, number of gears, type of bicycle (mountain bike, racing bike, boy's, girl's, man's, woman's).

Name _____
Date _____

Lost and found

Lost

Small brown and white dog. One ear missing. Walks with a slight limp. Part of tail missing. Answers to the name of Lucky.

Please tell Susan Carter at Brook Farm.

Found

Talking bird. Please hurry up and collect it. It knows some terrible words! Yellow and green with yellow patch around right eye. Seems to prefer milk to water. Loves looking in mirror. Eats anything and everything.

Will sell to pet shop if not claimed by Friday. Please tell Mrs Black at Rose Cottage.

▲ Can you use the space below to make up your own lost or found notice?

Suggestion(s) for extension

Children could write a story about how the bicycle came to be lost and found. Perhaps it was stolen, perhaps the owner left it somewhere and forgot about it, perhaps it was a magic bicycle which had a mind of its own and decided to run away from a careless owner.

Suggestion(s) for support

Ask children to dictate their ideas for descriptions of the bicycles to you or an adult helper and then provide them with a written outline which they may follow in their own writing.

Assessment opportunities

Look for evidence of appropriate use of vocabulary and concise descriptive writing.

Opportunities for IT

The children could use a word processor to write the lost and found notices. As the notices must be fairly short the text entry part of the activity should not take too long. The children could be set a word limit, perhaps 30 words, and be shown how to use the word count facility to check on the number of words used. They may need to edit and redraft their work to keep within the word limit.

Display ideas

The lost and found notices are best used for real audiences from other classes initially, but could then be displayed together with other work on bicycles.

Other aspects of the English PoS covered

Speaking and listening – 3b.
Reading – 2b.

Reference to photocopiable sheet

Photocopiable page 153 provides examples of lost and found notices. Space is provided for children to make up their own notice about a missing item.

LISTS

To write accurately for an audience and to make use of knowledge of sound–symbol correspondence.

†† *Whole class or group, working together initially and then individually or in pairs.*

🕐 *At least one hour.*

Key background information

A key feature of children's early writing is the making of lists (see *The Emergence of Literacy* by Nigel Hall, Hodder & Stoughton, 1987). In writing lists children make use of their growing understanding of sound–symbol correspondence and learn the importance of careful presentation for a real audience.

In this activity children are asked to make various lists. A starting point might be *Fascinating Lists* compiled by Rosemary Border (Henderson Publishing, 1990) in which a range of lists is provided.

Preparation

Decide upon a variety of different categories for the children's lists and write these on pieces of card. Put the pieces of card in a box.

Resources needed

Pieces of card, box to put cards in, chalkboard, simple dictionaries and reference books, photocopiable page 154, writing materials.

What to do

Talk with the children about lists. You might refer to shopping lists, particularly if they have already attempted the activity on page 90. Ask one child to come out and pick a card from the box of categories. Show this to the children and ask them for suggestions for items which could be written on a list to go with the category. Repeat the exercise until the children have understood the concept of lists. The following

categories might be useful:

Boys' names
Girls' names
Towns and cities
Countries
Trees
Dinosaurs
Birds
Teachers
Shops
Kings and queens
Cars
Names of pets
Favourite TV programmes
Favourite foods.

Give out photocopiable page 154. This provides an introductory activity which can be attempted by the children before they go on to work more independently on their own lists. The sheet includes lists for the children to complete and spaces for them to write the name of each category. There are also category headings with a limited number of items listed and spaces for the children to add to the lists.

The children might be encouraged to use simple dictionaries and wordbooks, as well as non-fiction books, to find items for their lists. Encourage them to look carefully at the words which they copy and stress the importance of careful spelling and presentation.

When the children have completed the photocopiable sheet, ask them to think of categories of their own or allow them to make use of those from the box. They may now work individually or in pairs to make further lists.

During the activity stop the children occasionally to read out, or ask the children to read out, the lists. Ask the children if they can add to the lists and make suggestions to help their classmates.

Suggestion(s) for extension

The activity may be extended in various ways including:

▲ children being asked to write sentences to include the names of the items on their lists;

▲ children trying to see how long a list they can make for each category;

▲ children rearranging their lists into alphabetical order.

Suggestion(s) for support

Some children may need to be provided with banks of words written on individual pieces of card. These could be discussed and then sorted into lists which the children could copy. They

might then be asked to think of further words for their lists and be helped to write these.

Assessment opportunities
Note the children's abilities to copy words accurately and look for evidence that they are developing an appreciation of sound–symbol correspondence when attempting to spell words independently.

Opportunities for IT
Some children could write their lists using a word processor. They could use the 'cut and paste' or 'drag and drop' facility to organise their lists into alphabetical order.

Display ideas
A book of lists could be made and then added to the class library. Each list could be left with spaces for readers to add further words.

Other aspects of the English PoS covered
Speaking and listening – 1a.
Reading – 1c; 2a, b, d.

Reference to photocopiable sheet
Photocopiable page 154 provides incomplete lists for children to think of appropriate words to add to them.

DIARY OF MY DAY

To write in sentences and use recording skills.
†† *Whole class or group, working individually or in pairs.*
🕐 *One hour initially, then ongoing.*

Key background information
In this activity the children write a sentence about what they have done at different times of the day.

Preparation
Prepare a brief diary of your own, describing what you have done at school during the previous day. Make copies of photocopiable page 155, one for each child.

Resources needed
Sample diary of a day, photocopiable page 155, chalkboard, writing materials.

What to do
At the beginning of the day explain to the children that they are going to keep a record of what they have done that day. Read to them the diary you have written of your previous day at school. Talk with the children about what you have included. Discuss the reasons for keeping a diary and tell them how useful the diaries of people like Samuel Pepys and Anne Frank have been in informing us about different times in history.

Ask the children to think about what they have done so far today and write some key words on the board. Then give out copies of photocopiable page 155 and explain to the children that they will each be completing their sheet at various times throughout the day. (The next time they write on the sheet could be just before or after the morning break.) Tell the children to write in sentences if they can, and emphasise the need to begin sentences with capital letters and end them with full stops. They should try to write one sentence for each section on the photocopiable sheet.

Within a few days of the activity, tell the children that they are going to keep a diary of the day again but that this time they are going to write two sentences each time. Explain that they should write about two different things and that one sentence should be written about each. They can write their sentences on a fresh copy of the photocopiable sheet.

Suggestion(s) for extension
Children might go on to produce diaries for days including what they have done outside school. The diaries might be kept over a longer period.

Suggestion(s) for support
Some children may find writing at length difficult. They could write single words or groups of words on the photocopiable sheet and perhaps draw accompanying pictures to illustrate what they have been doing, before working with you or another adult to produce some more detailed written work.

Assessment opportunities
Note the children's abilities to write in sentences and to adopt a diary format.

Opportunities for IT
Some of the children could write their diary using a word processor, giving them an opportunity to save their work and then retrieve it for the next entry. They could also be shown how to set out their diary, using headings or columns to separate the times from the actual entries. For example:

10.00 am I worked on my maths book
11.00 am I played in the playground

Display ideas
Diary entries could be compared and some children might produce reports on the day based upon the entries of the children in their group. These could be displayed alongside pictures of clocks which show the times of the different events.

Other aspects of the English PoS covered
Speaking and listening – 1c.
Reading – 1c.

Reference to photocopiable sheet
Photocopiable page 155 provides a framework for the children to use when writing a 'Diary of my day'. They can write in list form or write one or more sentences, depending on their abilities.

BIRTHDAY PARTY INVITATIONS

To write for an audience, showing awareness of the spellings of classmates' names and making use of presentational skills.

†† *Whole class or group, working individually or in pairs.*

🕐 *One hour.*

Key background information
In this activity children will make a list of the people whom they would like to invite to a birthday party. They will then go on to make invitations.

Preparation
If possible, acquire some commercially produced party invitations to show to the children. Children could be asked to bring invitations to school if they have recently attended a party. If possible, find some coloured brochures or pamphlets which give details of arrangements which can be made for parties – many fast food restaurants produce these.

Resources needed
Party invitations, brochures which give details of facilities for parties (optional), chalkboard, writing materials. Card for extension activity. Word bank for support activity.

What to do
Make a list on the board of people whom you would invite to a party. Include the names of some famous people and tell the children why you made your choices. Talk to the children about birthday parties and ask them to tell you about their own parties and who attended them. Often children have parties at leisure centres or restaurants rather than at home. Some parties have a theme such as a colour that everyone must wear or they may require fancy dress. Make a list of all the different kinds of parties which the children describe.

Talk with the children about what it is like to be invited to a party and about how they feel when they are not invited. Ask the children to imagine that they are going to have a party and to think carefully about the people whom they would like to invite to their parties. They might be told that, since the parties are imaginary, they could invite famous people as well as family and friends.

The children might be encouraged to think about themes and venues for their parties. If you have been able to obtain some brochures giving details of party arrangements, show these to the children.

Ask the children to make a list of people whom they would like to invite to their parties and then to make attractive invitations. Show the children some commercially produced invitations and explain that the invitations need to provide information so that the person invited knows when and where

the party is to be held, as well as details of when it will finish, perhaps what clothes should be worn and so on. Show them how they can use different handwriting styles for different parts of the invitation when they are writing their own invitations and stress the importance of presenting their work carefully and accurately.

Suggestion(s) for extension
Some children could go on to write letters of invitation in which they give details of the things which will happen at the party. They could tell the guest about the other guests who have been invited, as well as describing games and food.

Suggestion(s) for support
Provide lists of names and key words which may be useful in preparing invitations.

Assessment opportunities
Look for signs that children are able to copy names accurately and for evidence of careful presentation, with different forms of handwriting being used where appropriate.

Opportunities for IT
The children could use a word processor or desktop publishing package to write and present their birthday invitations. As the text entry is relatively short, attention can be focused on organising the information to create an interesting invitation, possibly using pictures and changing the font styles, sizes and colours.

Display ideas
Make a wall display of the children's invitations and continue the party theme with a display of paper hats, prizes, and so on set out on a table underneath the children's writing.

Other aspects of the English PoS covered
Speaking and listening – 1a.
Reading – 1c.

PARTY GAMES

To write instructions using complete sentences with capital letters and full stops and to develop chronological writing.

†† *Whole class or group, working in pairs.*

🕐 *One hour.*

Previous skills/knowledge needed
Children will need some knowledge of common party games.

Key background information
In this activity the children will write the instructions for party games. The activity may be ideal for the period leading up to Christmas parties, or it may be undertaken as part of a topic on birthdays.

Preparation
Since this activity involves writing instructions for party games it would be a good idea to introduce it by playing some of the games with the children.

Resources needed
Any resources which are used in the playing of party games, chalkboard, writing materials.

What to do
After playing party games with the children talk about the rules for each one. Ask them if they have ever played the games with different rules and discuss the variations.

Talk with the children about other games which they have played at parties and ask them to describe how each game is played. Write details of one or two games on the board.

You could begin by making a list of the instructions in note form and then asking the children to give you ideas for writing the instructions in more detail. Show the children how these can be written chronologically. When you have finished writing the instructions ask the children to tell you if the instructions are clear enough to help someone who had never heard of the game to be able to play it.

Ask the children to work in pairs to discuss how different games are played. When they have done this, ask them to write details of the way in which one game is played. Encourage them to begin by making a list on which they can build to write instructions in sentences. Remind the children to try to write their instructions in chronological order.

Explain to the children that their instructions may be needed by other children or teachers who are having parties, so it will be important to explain the rules and instructions very carefully and clearly.

Suggestion(s) for extension
Children might, under supervision, teach others how to play the games using their lists of rules and instructions to help them. Children should modify their written instructions when it becomes clear that others find them difficult to follow.

Suggestion(s) for support
Some children may need to begin by drawing simple pictures of the sequence of events before being helped with writing. Thoughtful pairings of children should enable those who find writing difficult to contribute ideas for their partner to write down. At a later stage the less able child might become more involved in the writing, perhaps through copying writing out for presentation.

Assessment opportunities
Note the children's abilities to use capital letters and full stops when writing sentences. Look for evidence that they can adopt an appropriate style for writing instructions. Note, too, their abilities to record instructions chronologically.

Opportunities for IT
The children could draft and present their rules using a word processor or desktop publishing package. They should be shown how to set the rules of their game out, possibly using tabs and other formatting commands, to position text on the page without using the space bar.

Display ideas
Children's instructions for games could be displayed without headings, with names of games displayed nearby. Other children could be invited to read the instructions and to match them to the names of the games.

Other aspects of the English PoS covered
Speaking and listening – 1a.

PARTY FOOD

To use lists and to organise work and present it in conjunction with pictures.

†† *Whole class or group, working individually or in pairs.*
🕐 *One hour.*

Key background information
In this activity the children will list the food which they would like to have at their birthday party. They may make use of early picture dictionaries and cuttings from magazines to help with spellings and to provide ideas. The activity may be ideal as a prelude to Christmas parties.

Preparation
Cut out pictures of food from newspaper supplements and colour magazines. Prepare a list of your own favourite party foods as a starting point for discussion.

Resources needed
Pictures of party food (see above), a list of your favourite foods, magazines containing articles on different kinds of food, picture dictionaries, chalkboard, writing materials.

What to do
Show the children some pictures of food and tell them about your favourite foods. Talk with the children about the food which they have eaten at parties and make a list of their favourite party foods. Write some of the names of foods on the board to provide guidance on spelling.

Ask the children to devise a menu for a party and list all the things which they would give their guests. Encourage them to look at magazines in which they may be able to find spellings. A discussion on healthy and less healthy foods could take place, although this is not the main reason for the activity.

Talk about party foods from around the world and discuss traditional dishes for celebrations. If possible, draw upon the knowledge of children from different ethnic groups and

cultures. Discuss the balance between sweet and savoury foods and talk about these terms with the children.

Encourage careful copying of words, perhaps using look–cover–write–check to foster close observation of word formation (Margaret Peters, 1985). Discuss sound–symbol correspondence where appropriate.

Ask the children to cut out pictures and label them as part of their lists.

Suggestion(s) for extension
Some children may go on to write recipes for some of the food items with the guidance of an adult helper.

Suggestion(s) for support
Children could work with partners to produce joint lists. Those children who experience difficulties in finding spellings from magazines could have a word list presented on a large sheet of paper which could be put on the wall near to their tables as a reference point.

Assessment opportunities
Note children's abilities to copy words accurately and their attempts at spelling using sound–symbol relationships.

Opportunities for IT
The children could write and present their party menu using a word processor or desktop publishing package. They could be shown how to format the text and alter the fonts and sizes to make the menu interesting to read. Pictures could be added, either taken from collections of clip art or drawn using an art package.

Display ideas
Party food lists could be displayed, together with a collection of packages for various party foods.

Other aspects of the English PoS covered
Speaking and listening – 1a; 2b.
Reading – 1c; 2d.

BIRTHDAY CARDS

To write for an audience using features of presentation.
†† *Whole class or group, working individually or in pairs.*
🕐 *One hour.*

Key background information
This activity makes use of a familiar genre as an example for children to follow. There is a real audience for the writing and an opportunity to discuss different modes of presentation with the children.

Preparation
Collect or save examples of birthday cards which contain a variety of messages inside them. Include some which have jokes or riddles and have a joke book in reserve in case the children run out of ideas.

Resources needed
A collection of birthday cards (see above), card, writing and drawing materials.

What to do
Show the children examples of birthday cards and ask them to find out the dates of the birthdays of members of their families and of friends. Talk with them about the next birthday which will be coming up among the people they know and explain that they are going to make a special card for that person. Alternatively, a member of staff or a friend of the school might be chosen by the children or yourself.

Ask the children what they think makes a good birthday card and what sort of things should be written on them. Discuss this while showing the children examples and reading them aloud. Compile a list of words which the children may draw upon when producing their own cards. Encourage them to think of more interesting captions than simply 'Happy birthday'.

Tell the children that they are going to make birthday cards and that they should think carefully about the people for whom they are making their cards. They should consider each person's hobbies and interests and decide if it would be a good idea to make a card which included these.

Tell the children that they will need to wish the person a happy birthday, but that they can also write other things on the card such as messages, verses, jokes or riddles. Show to the children the variety of content in the cards that you have in your collection.

Suggestion(s) for extension
Some children could look closely at the rhymes and messages in birthday cards and attempt to write their own. These could be done with the help of an adult or could be developed from rhymes started by you.

Suggestion(s) for support
Children who experience difficulty might be allowed to cut up old cards and stick parts of these on to card as a starting point for their own work.

Assessment opportunities
Observe children's attempts at copying words accurately and note their abilities to present work carefully and attractively.

Opportunities for IT
Children could use an art or drawing package to create pictures for their birthday cards, or they could select suitable pictures from a clip art collection. These can be imported into a drawing package and arranged to create a suitable picture. A message could then be added using appropriate fonts. Children could also use specific software such as *Clare's Cardshop* to design and print their cards.

Display ideas
Cards could be displayed on doors or walls by attaching string to the surface in a vertical line and then pegging cards to this.

Other aspects of the English PoS covered
Speaking and listening – 1a; 3b.
Reading – 1c; 2d.

DEVELOPING A WORD BANK

To write accurately using commonly used words and/ or words which are needed for a topic.
†† *Whole class or group.*
🕐 *Up to one hour, but the activity can be continued over a number of weeks.*

Key background information
This activity may be done as a one-off lesson, or it may be an ongoing activity. The objective is to enable the children to build up a bank of words which will help them with writing and spelling. The word bank may be for general use or it may be related to a topic. The activity is also designed to develop children's knowledge of the alphabet.

Preparation
If the word bank is to be used for a particular topic, make a preparatory list of words. Make an alphabet strip to help the children to try to sort words into alphabetical order. Make copies of photocopiable page 156 to use according to your particular needs.

Resources needed
Card-index box or folder for word-bank cards/sheets to be stored in (or wordbooks in which the word bank is written), alphabet strip, display board, card, Blu-Tack, cassette recorder and audio cassette of a conversation, writing materials. List of words related to a particular topic (optional), photocopiable page 156 (optional). Dictionaries and reference books for the extension activity.

What to do
If the word bank is to be for general use:
Ask the children to tell you which words they

A word bank

a	h	o	u
about	have	once	use
after	help	one	used
again	house	our	
			v
b	i	p	very
because	inside	people	
before		picture	w
	j		walk
	just	q	want
c		quick	watch
came	k	quiet	water
come	know		what
could		r	when
	l	ready	where
d	learn	right	who
do	like		why
does	little	s	would
down	love	said	write
		school	
e	m	should	y
each	many		year
every	minute	t	you
	much	talk	your
f		teacher	
first	n	their	
from	name	there	
	next	through	
g	nothing		
give			
goes			

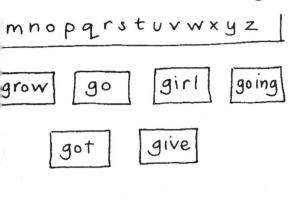

m n o p q r s t u v w x y z

| grow | go | girl | going |

| got | give |

use a lot in their writing. Write them on pieces of card and attach these to a display board as they tell you. Photocopiable page 156 provides a list of words which will be useful as a basic list. Play an audio cassette of a short extract of a conversation and ask the children to listen carefully and think about the words which people use a lot. Tell them to offer you suggestions.

If the word bank is to be related to a topic or theme:
Talk about the topic and ask the children to think about the different words which they will meet as they study it. Write the children's words on pieces of card and attach them to a board for reference. Help the children with their suggestions by using the word list that you have prepared.

When there are several words on the board, go through the alphabet with the children. (Fix an alphabet strip to the top of the board as an aide-mémoire.) Ask the children which word should come first if the words are arranged in alphabetical order. Explain that we look at the first letters of the words to decide the order and that, if these are the same, we look at the second and third letters and so on. Let the children help you to arrange the words in alphabetical order.

Tell the children that the list is not complete and that as they meet new words these can be added. The word bank may be presented in different ways:
▲ Each child could copy the words into an alphabetically arranged wordbook. This might be one of the commercially produced booklets.
▲ Each child could copy the list on to a sheet of paper which could be placed in a topic book for easy reference.
▲ The words could be available on a display board as a central reference point to encourage children to visit when they needed words and to use the look–cover–write–check method of learning them (Margaret Peters, 1985).
▲ The words could be placed in a card index box, in alphabetical order, for reference.

Suggestion(s) for extension
Those children who are capable of doing so could use dictionaries to help them to find additional words. They might also use reference books to find words which will help them for a particular topic.

Suggestion(s) for support
Some children will need to concentrate on simple, phonically regular or common words at first. The number of 'new' words should be limited for these children and care should be taken to ensure that they are able to read all of their words.

Assessment opportunities
Note the children's abilities to copy words accurately and look for signs that children are holding pencils comfortably and are forming letters correctly. Look, too, for evidence that children understand alphabetical order.

Display ideas
A central display with words written on cards and attached to a notice-board can be a useful resource and a valuable aid to learning if the children are encouraged to add to it and place new words correctly in alphabetical order.

Other aspects of the English PoS covered
Speaking and listening – 3a, b.
Reading – 2a.

Reference to photocopiable sheet
Photocopiable page 156 provides a list of words to be used as a word bank in the activity if the words are to be for general use rather than related to a particular topic or theme.

TREASURE HUNTS

To write for an audience.
†† *Group of four children.*
🕐 *One hour.*

Key background information
In this activity the teacher prepares a treasure hunt for the children who then prepare their own. In a treasure hunt, clues are written and hidden to lead treasure seekers to a prize. Often, the clues are written in verse and they may be cryptic.

It is important that care is taken to hide clues in safe places and to make sure that children know that none will be found near electrical sockets, or in places which would normally be out of bounds or which might require them to climb.

Preparation
Prepare a set of clues which can be secreted in different parts of the classroom and which eventually lead to treasure in the form of a small prize. As a rough guide, six clues are probably sufficient. Photocopiable page 157 provides clues which could be used in many classrooms but which could be adapted to meet the needs of the children and the contents of the classroom. Make a copy of the sheet and cut out the clues. Then hide each clue in its appropriate place in the classroom.

Resources needed
Sample treasure clues, small prizes, photocopiable page 157, A3 paper, writing materials.

What to do
Show the children sample clues for a treasure hunt and explain that the clues lead one from place to place until the treasure is found. Explain that clues can be written in rhyming couplets. The sample clues should be written on large sheets of paper so that everyone can read them.

Explain that you have hidden a number of clues in the classroom and that you would like the children to try to find them. It may be a good idea to limit the treasure seekers to four and to let them try the treasure hunt when the other children are outside playing. In this way the treasure hunt could be repeated by other children without the clues being given away.

Give the first clue to the treasure seekers and let each child read it. The children might compete with each other to find the treasure first or they could co-operate to find treasure which could be shared.

When the children have completed the treasure hunt ask them to try to devise a treasure hunt of their own. Tell the children that their clues do not have to be written in rhyme if they do not wish. Remind them that when they write clues they must not name the place where the clue can be found, but must give information which will lead to its discovery. Explain that there are some places in which they must not place clues and that the clues for the treasure hunt must be confined to a certain area. This might be the classroom or it could be the school grounds. Tell the children that you want to see their clues so that you can check that they are suitable and that they do not lead treasure hunters into places where they should not go.

When the children have completed their treasure hunts ask them to hide the clues and let other members of the class try to find the treasure.

Suggestion(s) for extension
Some children may be able to devise longer and more complex treasure hunts and may even be able to produce clues which take the form of rhyming couplets. In treasure hunts these rhymes can be rather trite but this adds to the fun!

Suggestion(s) for support
Some children may need to draw pictures rather than write words for clues. They could be encouraged to draw a picture and write one or two words with the help of a partner or an adult.

Assessment opportunities
Note children's abilities to communicate effectively in writing information which is helpful to the purpose, task and reader.

Display ideas
A display of treasure-hunt clues could be put on the wall, together with a plan of the part of the school which they refer to.

Other aspects of the English PoS covered
Speaking and listening – 1b.
Reading – 1b.

Reference to photocopiable sheet
Photocopiable page 157 provides a sample treasure hunt which could easily be adapted for use in most classrooms.

LETTER TO PARENTS

To use a format for letter writing and to write for an audience.

†† *Whole class or group, working as individuals.*

🕐 *At least one hour.*

Key background information
In this activity children write to their parents to tell them about the things that they do at school. The activity might be seen as a precursor to personal profiles.

Preparation
Write a letter which explains all of the things which you, as a teacher, do at school. Children may be surprised to learn that you spend a long time working before they arrive and after they go home.

Resources needed
Letter describing your day at school, envelopes, chalkboard, writing materials.

What to do
Read your letter to the children. It could be addressed to your own parents, to a relative or to a friend. Talk with the children about what you have written and ask them if anything surprised them.

Many children when asked by their parents what they have done at school answer 'Nothing'. Tell the children that you want them to write to their parents and tell them all about the different things which they do at school. Before the children begin to write, a brainstorming session with the whole class or group might help to provide ideas. They could be asked to mention different things which they do at school and these could be written on the board to provide ideas and a word bank.

Talk with the children about the structure of a letter and explain that they should write the school's address at the top of the page and the date and that they should begin their letters 'Dear...' Since they are writing to their parents it would be inappropriate to use 'Yours sincerely' at the end and children might instead sign their letters 'Love from...' Parents might like to compare what the children do with what they did when they were pupils of the same age. The children could include questions at the end of their letters asking parents about their own school days. It is important here to

be sensitive to the difficulties of any parents who may have literacy problems.

Completed letters could be read aloud to the class, before being sent to parents with an accompanying note from you explaining the activity and inviting parents to write their own letters answering the children's questions and providing a description of their own schooldays.

Suggestion(s) for extension
A senior citizen could be invited to the school to talk with the children and answer their questions about his or her own schooldays. The children could prepare questions in advance and write these down to help them to remember them. Alternatively, they could write to the visitor in advance of the visit.

Suggestion(s) for support
Some children could make lists of things which they do at school and draw pictures of them. You could write letters from some children on the board or on a large piece of paper, with lots of contributions from the children. The children could then copy the letters to send to parents.

Assessment opportunities
Look for signs that children are able to follow the letter format and are able to write for an audience. Note, too, their use of question marks.

Opportunities for IT
The children could write their letter using a word processor. They should be shown how to position parts of the letter using appropriate commands. To speed up the activity you could prepare and save a template with the address already entered, although not formatted, so that the children could load the letter file, format the address and then focus on the content of the letter.

Display ideas
Parents' replies could be displayed for children to read.

Other aspects of the English PoS covered
Speaking and listening – 1b, c.
Reading – 1a.

 PEN-PALS

To use letter writing for a real audience.
✝✝ *Whole class or group, working individually or in pairs.*
🕐 *One hour.*

Key background information
In this activity children write to pen-pals. The activity is designed to develop letter writing and the use of question marks and capital letters.

Preparation
Arrange with a friend from another school for a pen-pal exchange of letters. Try to find out about the children in each other's classes so that suitable pairings may be made. Prepare a sample letter to a pen-pal.

Resources needed
Example of a letter to a pen-pal, chalkboard, large envelope, writing materials.

What to do
Show the children the sample letter you have written and talk with them about its features. Discuss the way in which questions are asked and information is given.

Explain that they are going to have pen-pals to whom they will write letters. Tell them that you have tried very hard to find for them a pen-pal who has similar interests or whom you think they would like. Talk about the sorts of things which they would like to tell their pen-pals about themselves and list some of these on the board.

Discuss the kinds of things which the children might like to know about their pen-pals and write some sample questions on the board, drawing the children's attention to the correct use of capital letters and question marks.

Encourage the children to draft their letters and explain that they should try to create a good impression upon their pen-pal by producing a neat, well-presented final copy of their letter to send. During the drafting stages help the children with spellings and draw everyone's attention to words which are required frequently. Discuss examples of interesting letters with the whole class and remind them about the way in which a letter should be set out.

When the children have completed their letters, place them in a single large envelope for posting. It is important that interest is maintained and early replies should be arranged.

When the replies arrive it will add to interest and excitement if the children open the envelope and see the letters themselves before you do. The letters could be discussed after the children have read them and everyone could take a turn to tell the rest of the class an interesting thing about his or her pen-pal.

Children's enthusiasm will be maintained if they are allowed to respond to the letters as soon as possible. They might spend time thinking about their replies over a day or two and making notes in preparation for writing letters.

Suggestion(s) for extension
Some children could write stories for their pen-pals or describe local places of interest. They might be asked in a brainstorming session to think about all of the things in the area which a visitor might like to see. They could then choose two or three of these and write brief descriptions informing their pen-pals about them.

Suggestion(s) for support
Those children who experience great difficulty with writing might dictate their letters to an adult helper and then copy the writing to send to their pen-pal.

Assessment opportunities
Note the children's abilities to appreciate that they are writing for an audience and to present their work in an appropriate way.

Opportunities for IT
If the letter writing is extended over a period of time, every child could have a turn at writing a letter using the word processor. They should be shown how to lay out and position different parts of the letter, such as the address, using appropriate formatting commands. Where schools have access to e-mail through the Internet, children could write their letters and send them electronically.

Display ideas
Letters received from pen-pals could be displayed so that everyone could see them. An alternative approach to the activity could be to have the other school write first, display the letters and ask the children to choose their pen-pals by reading the letters displayed.

Other aspects of the English PoS covered
Speaking and listening – 1c.
Reading – 1c.

DO THEY KNOW IT'S CHRISTMAS?

To produce independent writing in response to a discussion about a familiar institution.

†† *Whole class or group, working individually or in pairs.*

🕐 *At least one hour.*

Key background information

In this activity children consider the meaning of Christmas and what Christmas means to them. They are encouraged to write about Christmas for someone who knows nothing of the way in which they celebrate it. Those children who are from religions which do not celebrate Christmas might still discuss Christmas, but could be asked to write about a special festival from their own faith.

Preparation

If possible, find a CD or tape of the song 'Do they know it's Christmas?' by Band Aid and books about Christmas customs and festivals. Bring photographs showing Christmas time to school and items such as Christmas cards, a wrapped 'present', a mince pie, a cracker, a recording of some carols and any other Christmas artefacts.

Resources needed

A recording of the song 'Do they know it's Christmas?' (see above), books about Christmas customs, various items associated with Christmas (see above), writing materials.

What to do

Tell the children that you are going to play them a song which some of them may have heard before and that you want them to listen very carefully to the words. Explain that the song was written especially to raise money to help people who were starving in Ethiopia and that the words ask if those people knew that it was Christmas at all.

Discuss with the children what Christmas means to them and ask them to describe the things which they do at Christmas time. Show the children the different Christmas artefacts and discuss them. Ask the children to suggest other things which they associate with Christmas. Tell them that you would like them to imagine that they were writing about Christmas for someone who did not know anything about it. It might be for someone from another country where people do not celebrate Christmas or it could even be for an alien from another planet! Talk with them about the things which they would need to explain and the ways in which they could do this.

Ask the children to jot down their ideas in note form before they begin to write in prose. Encourage them to see their notes as temporary and tell them that they may add to them and that they do not have to use all of them in their final draft.

Suggestion(s) for extension

Some children might write a plan for a class assembly in which they tell the rest of the school about the ways in which they celebrate Christmas. They could write a running order for the assembly detailing who should do what and when.

Suggestion(s) for support

Children may need the support of a framework plan for their writing. This might take the form of a series of headings such as:

▲ We celebrate Christmas because...

▲ At Christmas we eat...

▲ At Christmas we give...

▲ At Christmas we see...

▲ I like Christmas time because...

Assessment opportunities

Note the children's abilities to write independently drawing upon personal experience. Note, too, their abilities to make use of their notes as a basis for their final drafts.

Display ideas

Children's writing could be mounted on boxes wrapped in Christmas paper and placed next to a class Christmas tree, which has been decorated with various items associated with Christmas.

Other aspects of the English PoS covered

Speaking and listening – 1c.

FIRST DAY AT SCHOOL

To write about personal experiences and to organise writing appropriately.

†† *Whole class or group, working individually.*

🕐 *At least one hour.*

Key background information

In this activity children are asked to recall their first day at school and write about it. The writing may take the form of an entry for a journal or it may be a brochure for new pupils to read or have read to them.

The activity should enable you to assess children's progress in a number of aspects of writing.

Preparation

It may be possible for you to provide photographs of the children's first day at school. These might be taken of the current reception class or may be requested from parents, some of whom may have taken pictures to record the event.

Resources needed

The poem 'First Day at School' by Roger McGough from *Autumn* by J. Wilson (McDonald, 1991). Photographs of the children's first day at school (optional), writing materials.

What to do

Talk with the children about what you remember of your own first day at school and ask them to recall their own. Read the poem by Roger McGough and discuss it with the children.

Explain that you would like them to write about their first day at school so that new pupils will know what to expect when they visit the school before starting formally. Tell them that you will put their writing into a book which can be read to the new children.

Encourage the children to begin by making simple notes to provide a plan for their work. This should enable you to provide a list of some of the spellings which they may need.

Ask them to work independently and encourage them to 'have a go' at spellings which they are unsure of, explaining that you will help them later.

Suggestion(s) for extension

Children might record their work on to tape so that it could be played to new pupils and to their parents. Alternatively, children could plan an ideal first day at school. They could think about any problems which they or other children experienced on their first day and could write suggestions for things which the school could do to help new pupils.

Suggestion(s) for support

Some children may need help from an adult. Note the extent to which help is given. If a vocabulary list is provided, look for signs that children are able to copy words accurately.

Assessment opportunities

Look for evidence that children are able to work independently and are able to use their notes to help them to plan and structure their work. Note their knowledge of sound–symbol correspondence when they attempt spellings and look for evidence that they are able to form letters correctly.

Opportunities for IT

Each child could write about his or her first day at school using a word processor. The final drafts could be printed out and bound as a class book.

A more ambitious project would be to use authoring software to create a multimedia presentation in which the children wrote about their first day. Pictures of the children could be scanned from actual photographs, or taken from a Kodak CD-ROM which had photos of each child in the class. The children could even record their own voices reading about their first day.

Display ideas

The writing might be placed in a book to be read to new children. An assembly could be held, in which McGough's poem and the children's work could be read aloud and discussed. If a tape recording has been made this could be placed next to the children's writing so that new children and parents might listen to it when they are being shown around the school.

Other aspects of the English PoS covered

Speaking and listening – 1a.

Reading – 1a, d.

Photocopiables

The pages in this section can be photocopied for use in the classroom or school which has purchased this book, and do not need to be declared in any return in respect of any photocopying licence.

They comprise a varied selection of both pupil and teacher resources, including pupil worksheets, resource material and record sheets to be completed by the teacher or children. Most of the photocopiable pages are related to individual activities in the book; the name of the activity is indicated at the top of the sheet, together with a page reference indicating where the lesson plan for that activity can be found. Many of the worksheets include instructions for the children but on the earlier sheets beginner readers are not expected to be able to read them; the focus should be on their writing skills.

Individual pages are discussed in detail within each lesson plan, accompanied by ideas for adaptation where appropriate – of course, each sheet can be adapted to suit your own needs and those of your class. Sheets can also be coloured, laminated, mounted on to card, enlarged and so on where appropriate.

Pupil worksheets and record sheets have spaces provided for children's names and for noting the date on which each sheet was used. This means that, if so required, they can be included easily within any pupil assessment portfolio.

People on the bus

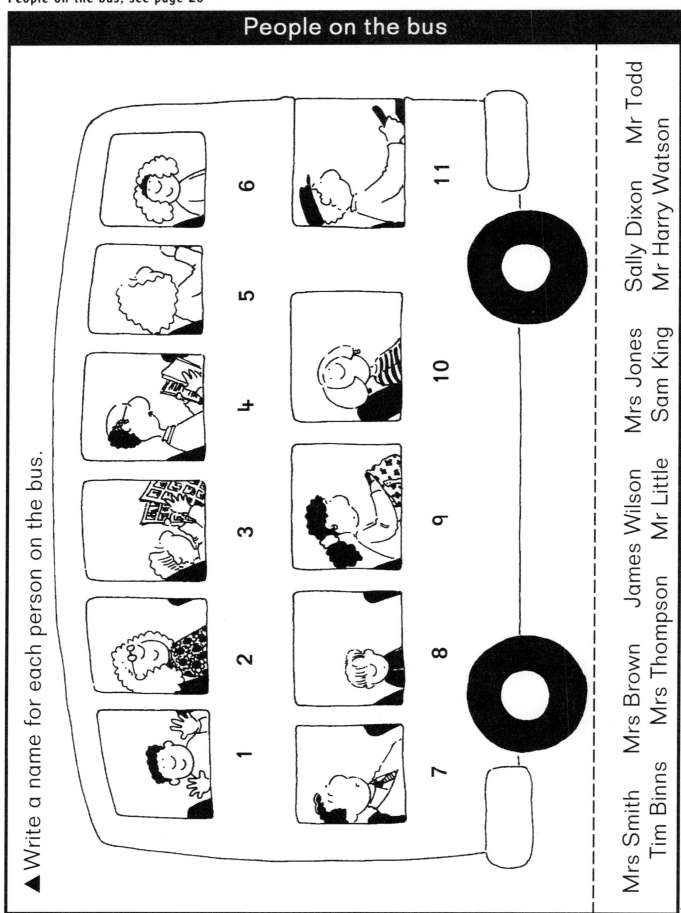

▲ Write a name for each person on the bus.

Mrs Smith   Mrs Brown   James Wilson   Mrs Jones   Sally Dixon   Mr Todd
Tim Binns   Mrs Thompson   Mr Little   Sam King   Mr Harry Watson

Photocopiables

Name _____

Date _____

▲ Stick a colour on each box. Write down things you can find in each colour under the boxes.

grey

green

blue

red

white

brown

orange

yellow

The washing-line, see page 23

The washing-line

▲ Which clothes do you think belong to each person?

baby Amy

Beth

Andrew

Mr Jaggs

Mrs Jaggs

Photocopiables

The street

Name_____   **Date**_____

▲ Colour each house a different colour.

Mrs Frank Mr Clark Miss Cox Miss Nash Mr Wong Mrs Bussell

▲ Write in the spaces the names of the people and the colours of the houses.

_____ lives in the _____ house.

_____ lives in the _____ house.

_____ lives in the _____ house.

_____ lives in the _____ house.

_____ lives in the _____ house.

_____ lives in the _____ house.

Pets and owners, see page 25

Pets and owners

Name _____   Date _____

Mr Green Jessica Brown David Black Emma Hampton Sarah Wilson Bill Davies

Book race (1)

bl	br	cl
cr	dr	fl
fr	gr	pl
pr	sc	sh
sk	sl	sm
sn	sp	st
sw	th	tr
tw	ai	aw
oa	oi	or
ou	ow	ar
or	ew	ch
au	all	wh

Book race, see page 27

Book race (2)

an	un	dis
ful	tion	ing
ed	ous	ies
con	ly	er

Capital letters (1)

Name _____   **Date** _____

▲ Look at the words on this sheet. Some of them should begin with capital letters. Find the words which need capital letters and write them correctly in the space under each word. Then write why the word needs a capital letter. The first word has been done for you.

london	scotland	city	wales
London	....	....	....
place	....	....	....

whales	i	me	man
....	....	....	....
....	....	....	....

mountain	ben nevis	france	country
....	....	....	....
....	....	....	....

friday	april	month	james
....	....	....	....
....	....	....	....

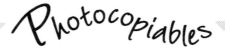

Capital letters, see page 31

Capital letters (2)

Name _____   Date _____

▲ This story has no capital letters. Read it carefully and then circle the words which you think should begin with a capital letter.

once upon a time there were three bears. there was a daddy bear, mummy bear and baby bear and they all lived together in a little house in the woods.

one day, just after daddy bear had made some porridge for breakfast, mummy bear said, 'let's go out for a little walk until the porridge has cooled', so they all set off into the woods.

while they were gone a little girl, called goldilocks, crept into their house and began to look around. she saw three bowls of porridge and tried each one before eating all of baby bear's.

goldilocks felt tired after eating so much porridge, so she decided to sit down. she tried two big chairs, but she did not like them. then she tried a little chair which belonged to baby bear, but when she sat on it the chair broke and she fell on to the floor.

goldilocks felt very sore after her fall, but she still climbed the stairs to the bears' bedroom. there were three beds and she tried lying on each one. she decided that she liked the small one best and she lay down and put her head on the pillow. very soon goldilocks fell asleep.

▲ How does the story end? Can you write the ending? Make sure you use capital letters in the right places.

Making sentences, see page 33

Making sentences (1)

Name _____   Date _____

▲ Can you join the parts of sentences to make complete
sentences? One has been done for you.

The snowball	a bone in its mouth.
The dog had	high in the sky.
The aeroplane flew	in my pocket.
I found 20 pence	was cold and wet.
Sita could not find	and started to cry.
Luke kicked the ball	her favourite doll.
Adam sat on the floor	through the window.
Heather and Sophie	were best friends.
It was a hot day	when the lion roared.
Everyone was afraid	and the sun shone.

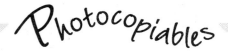
Making sentences (2)

Name _____   Date _____

▲ Use the parts of sentences as many times as you like to make as many sentences as you can. Write your sentences on paper.

The big, black car	was good at dancing.
A white horse	drove up the hill.
A ginger cat	did not like carrots.
Rebecca Smart	loved to eat carrots.
Simon and Peter	stood a silver fairy.
The young girl	it was dark and cold.
On top of the tree	liked reading books.
Inside the cave	hid under the chair.
A little mouse	keeps you warm.
A woollen hat	is an animal.

Commas

Name _____ Date _____

▲ Can you put commas in the right places?

Miss Jones had a big blue fast car.

Dean was tall dark and noisy.

Emma played football hockey tennis and netball.

It was dark damp and dusty in the old grey empty house.

▲ Can you write sentences which describe the children?
There are some words to help you underneath the pictures.

Simon	Jenny	Mark	Nicola
clever	cross	polite	cheerful
happy	naughty	friendly	helpful
content	unhappy	gentle	lucky

No more Mr Nice Guy, see page 37

A nice day

Name _____ **Date** _____

In the summer I had a really nice time when we went to the seaside.

The sky was blue and it was a really nice day. After a nice easy

drive we reached Bridlington at 10 o'clock in the morning.

When we had parked the car in a nice street we walked to the

beach. The sand was nice and clean, and the sea was a nice deep

blue colour. We made sandcastles and Mum bought us some nice

flags to stick into them. My sister had a nice time burying my dad in

the sand until only his head could be seen. I can't wait to see the

photographs!

On the way home we stopped at a café and had some really nice

cakes and a nice cold drink and Mum and Dad had a nice cup of tea.

Coded messages

Name _____   **Date** _____

▲ Can you put the words in the right order and then answer the questions?

name is What your?

old you How are?

name teacher What the is of your?

day today What is it?

brothers Do have you sisters and any?

name school your What the is of?

try Now to write sentences jumbled your own of.

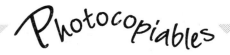
Opposites

Name _____   **Date** _____

▲ Look at the sentences and then try to write a sentence which means the opposite of each one.

The tall man was sitting smiling.

It was a lovely, sunny day with a clear blue sky.

David was very good at football.

The big boy was playing outside.

I was very unhappy when I lost my ballet shoes.

The winter days are short, cold and dark.

Alice hit the ball and it flew high into the air.

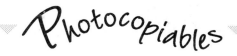

Homonyms

Name _____ **Date** _____

▲ Can you choose the right word to put into each sentence?

1 We had to .... a long time for the bus. (wait/weight)

2 He did not .... the answer to the question. (no/know)

3 Indra thought she .... a ghost when she woke up. (saw/sore)

4 Steven had .... T-shirts. (for/four)

▲ Now read the story and see if you can choose the right words to fill in the spaces.

It was a dark and windy .... (knight/night). The Hobbs family had decided to .... (sale/sail) to France in the dark. James and Kate sat in the cabin and .... (ate/eight) some biscuits and drank cocoa.

Suddenly ....(there/their) was a loud crashing sound. The children ran up the .... (stares/stairs) to the deck to .... (sea/see) what had happened. 'I must have fallen asleep!' called their .... (farther/father). 'We .... (seem/seam) to have hit a rock.'

Just then .... (there/their) mother climbed over the side of the boat and on to the deck. She was soaking wet. 'It's all .... (write/right),' she said. 'The boat doesn't have a .... (whole/hole) in it and anyway, we will be on the .... (beech/beach) soon.'

The sun rose and the children saw that there were houses nearby. 'Now there is just one thing to worry about,' said .... (their/there) father. 'Are we in France or are we in England?'

Subject–verb agreement

Name _____   **Date** _____

▲ Look at the example of a three-year-old child talking to her father and try to identify her mistakes. Write what Sarah should have said on each line.

Sarah: Jane be over there, Daddy.

_____

Father: Oh, yes, I can see her.

Sarah: Why did her go there, Daddy?

_____

Father: She went to get a cake.

Sarah: You given her one?

_____

Father: Yes, I did.

Sarah: And Jane comed for a cake.

_____

Super Sal, see page 45

Super Sal and the sprouts (1)

'But I hate sprouts!' cried Sally as she looked down at the five green vegetables on her plate.

'You know the rule,' said Mrs Ball. 'You sit there until you have a clean plate.'

Sally Ball pulled a face at her mother's back as Mrs Ball left the room. She stared miserably at the Brussels sprouts. 'Perhaps I could hide them somewhere,' she thought, but then she remembered the trouble there had been when her mother had found the carrots she had hidden behind the piano last year.

After a few minutes, Sally picked up her fork and stabbed a sprout. There was a bowl of sugar on the table and this gave her an idea. She went to the door and checked that Mum was not outside and then dipped the sprout in the sugar and popped it into her mouth. She chewed it quickly and swallowed. It was not too bad so she did the same with the rest of the sprouts and sat back feeling a little sick, but happy that the ordeal was over.

At that moment her mother walked into the room. 'Sally Ball, where are you?' she called as she stood in the doorway. 'That little madam! If she's sneaked out to play and hidden those sprouts there'll be trouble.'

'I'm here Mum,' said Sally wondering why her mother did not seem to be able to see her.

'Sally!' shouted Mrs Ball, 'Come back here this minute!'

'I am here,' cried Sally and she stood right in front of her mother.

'Tony, Stephen, Richard,' yelled Mrs Ball, 'Have any of you seen Sally?'

'Stop being silly Mum, I'm here,' insisted Sally, but her mother took no notice.

Sally began to wonder if her mother was playing a joke or if she really could not see her. When Mrs Ball went out of the room, Sally went to the mirror above the sideboard. She stood on tiptoes to look at herself, but she did not seem to be able to make herself tall enough to see her reflection. She moved one of the dining chairs and stood on that, but still she could see no reflection in the mirror. When she looked down at her hands she could see them perfectly clearly. In fact she could see her legs and feet too, but, when she leaned over and put her hand right next to the mirror, there was no reflection at all.

Super Sal and the sprouts (2)

'That chair has moved! It wasn't there when I left the room,' shrieked Mrs Ball as she entered the room followed by Mr Ball. 'She's hiding in here somewhere.'

Sally stood in front of her father and waved her hands in the air, but he ignored her completely. 'Come on out Sally,' he said as he peered around the room, 'you've had your little joke now.'

'I'm here Dad, look,' called Sally, but still no one seemed able to see or hear her.

'Come on Dad,' said Richard, 'the silly little thing will come out soon enough. Let's make the most of a bit of peace while she's hiding.'

This was too much for Sally. She marched over to Richard and pinched his arm. 'Ow!' he yelled, 'who did that?' He turned to Stephen, but he was behind Mrs Ball so it couldn't have been him. His father was at the other side of the room and his mother surely wouldn't pinch him. Sally trod on his foot and he yelled once more. 'Mum, someone's attacking me!'

'Don't be so daft, Richard, it's bad enough having a silly daughter without you being a fool as well,' stormed Mr Ball and Richard decided it would be best not to say anything else.

'So they can feel me even if they can't see or hear me,' thought Sally. 'Those sprouts must have made me invisible. Perhaps eating them with sugar wasn't such a good idea after all.' She thought again and began to wonder if being invisible might be rather fun. Sally picked up the bowl of sugar and Stephen gasped. 'Mum, Dad, look. The sugar bowl is flying!' The family stared in amazement as the bowl swayed about in the air above the table. The spoon dipped into the white grains and flew towards Stephen. It hovered above his head for a moment and then the sugar sprinkled over his fair hair as he tried to wriggle away from it.

Next to the telephone was a box of chocolate eggs. As the family stood gaping with disbelief, Sally decided to eat one to take away the taste of the sugary sprouts. As she bit into the egg and munched the thick, rich chocolate coating and slurped the creamy middle, she saw her mother's expression change from puzzlement to alarm. 'It's... you're... I can see you!' she stammered. 'Sally, what on earth have you been doing?'

'Well, Mum...' began Sally.

'Now just think carefully before you speak, Sally Ball,' said her mother. 'You know I can see right through you when you tell lies!'

Super Sal, see page 45

Super Sal: language study assessment sheet

Name:		Age:	Date:

Languages spoken:

Comment on the child's ability to:

⌒⌒ plan and review writing	
⌒⌒ write fluently and accurately	
⌒⌒ use full stops appropriately	
⌒⌒ use commas appropriately	
⌒⌒ use question marks appropriately	
⌒⌒ use capital letters appropriately	
⌒⌒ spell commonly occurring simple words correctly	
▲ use knowledge of sound–symbol correspondence in spelling	
▲ present work legibly	
▲ use dictionaries etc. to help with spelling	
▲ make interesting and appropriate vocabulary choices	

Pictures of people, see page 48

Pictures of people

Name _____   Date _____

Happy charts, see page 50

Happy charts

Name _____   Date _____

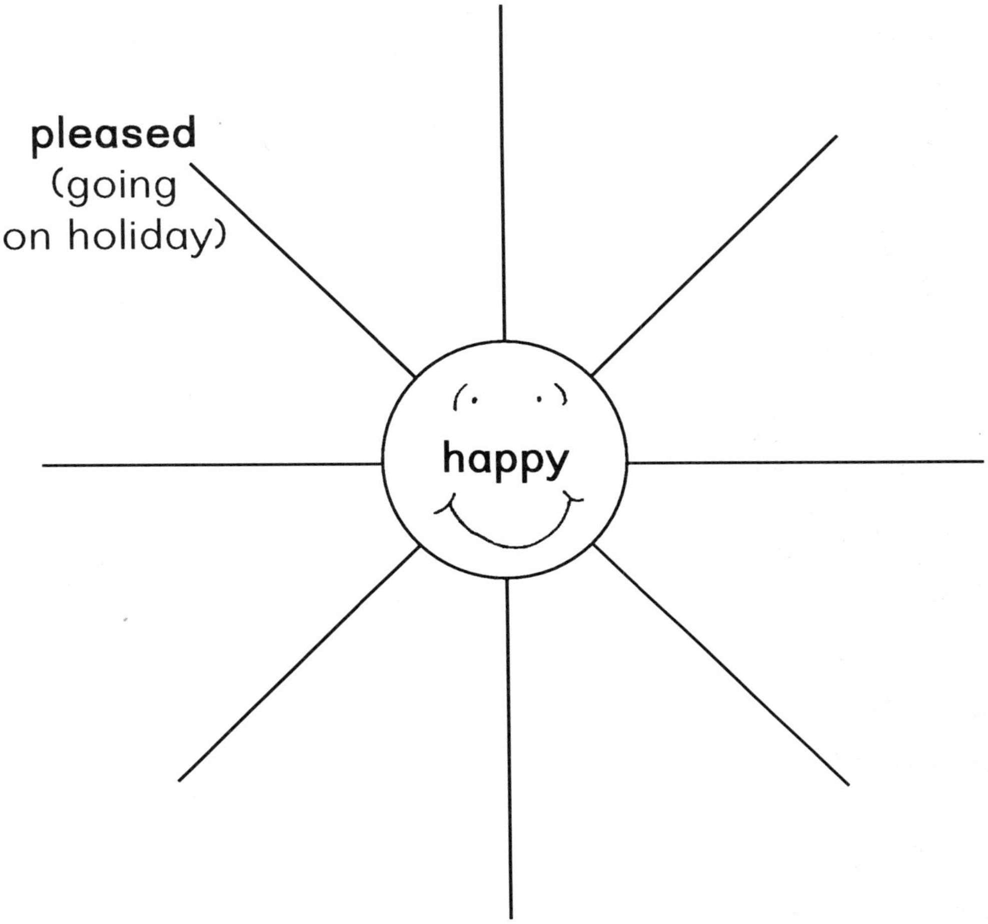

pleased
(going
on holiday)

happy

A letter to Santa Claus, see page 52

A letter from Santa Claus

Dear

I hope that you are well and that you are looking forward to Christmas.

I am always very busy at this time of the year. There are so many jobs to do. I have to clean and polish the sleigh and groom the reindeer. Then there are all those presents to sort out. I hardly have time to stop for something to eat. Mind you, I have been trying not to eat too much. I am beginning to get a bit too fat to get down some of the chimneys!

Have you been busy finding presents for your family? What would you like to give to them? Last year I received two hundred and fifty bottles of aftershave. I wouldn't mind, but I have a beard!

Do you know what you would like for Christmas? Perhaps you could tell me when you write to me. I would like some warm socks and some thick gloves. It's very cold sitting on that sleigh in the middle of winter!

This year I have a new reindeer. I haven't thought of a name for him yet. Do you have any ideas? I'd love to hear them if you do.

Well, I suppose I had better get back to work. Please write to me and tell me all about yourself and your family and friends. I would love to hear from you.

Merry Christmas

Santa

The scarecrow, see page 55

The scarecrow

Name _____   Date _____

I am a scarecrow. My name is _____

I live...   I can see...

I can hear...   I can smell...

A plan of a story

Name _____   **Date** _____

Think about your story and use the headings to make a plan.
▲ Where does the story take place?

▲ Who are the most important people in the story?

▲ Write about the three most interesting things which happen in the story.

1

2

3

▲ What happens at the end of the story? You can use the back of this sheet.

A class trip

It was the day of the trip to York and everyone was looking cross. Samantha and Amrit looked at each other and sighed. Ben started to sing 'Why are we waiting', but Mrs Mitchell told him to be quiet. Everyone in the classroom was miserable because the bus was late.

Suddenly Stephen jumped up and called, 'Mrs Mitchell, it's here. I can hear it coming!'

'Quiet everyone,' said Mrs Mitchell. 'Let's listen carefully and see if Stephen is right.' Sure enough, the sound of the bus could be heard getting louder as it got nearer to the school. 'Right, Kirsty's table line up at the door please,' said Mrs Mitchell. She then asked the children from the other tables to join them and they were ready to go. At least everyone except Mike was ready. He was still looking for his notebook so Mrs Mitchell asked Ross to help him.

At last they got on the bus and Mrs Mitchell and Mr Gray, who was coming along to help, together with Joseph's mother and William's mother, counted everyone twice to make sure that no one would be left behind. Katherine had left her packed lunch in the classroom so she had to run back and get it, but the bus finally managed to leave only half an hour late. Everyone was excited and Richard and Chris, who were sitting on the back seat, began to sing.

'Not yet, not yet!' shouted Mrs Mitchell. 'You may sing on the way home. Right now you should be looking at the worksheets which I gave to you to fill in on the journey.' Lisa and Ryan stopped writing in the mist on the window and looked at their worksheets.

'I bet I can finish mine before you,' said Lisa.

'I bet you can't,' said Ryan.

'Bet I can,' said Lisa.

'No you can't,' said Ryan.

'Excuse me,' said Mr Gray, firmly. 'I think you two should stop arguing about who is going to finish first and get started!'

Fantasy Island, see page 60

Fantasy Island (1)

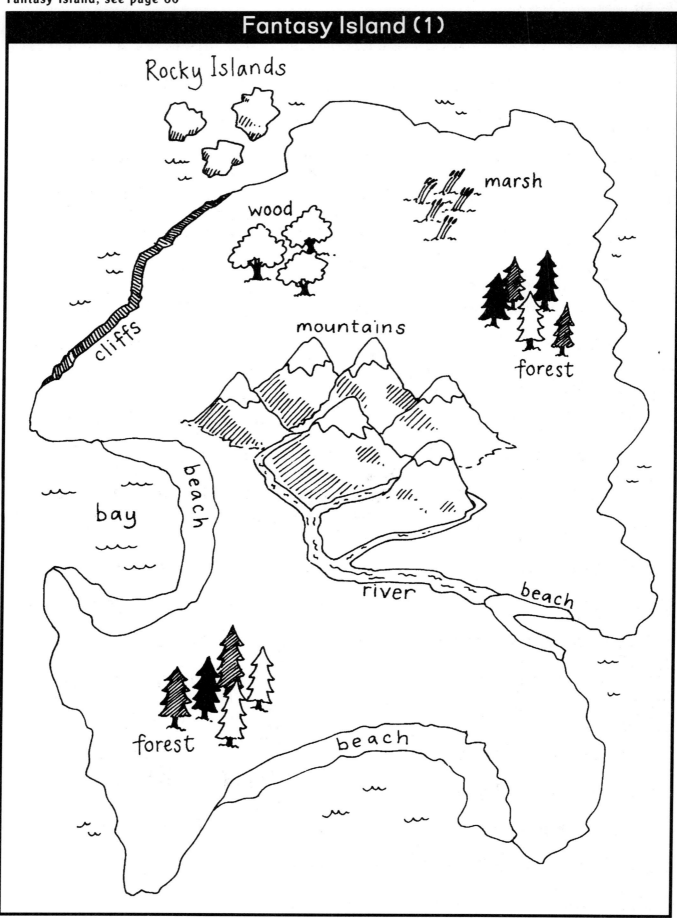

Fantasy Island (2)

The waves crashed against the side of the boat as we made our way towards the island. _____ had been the first to see land. She had called out 'Land ahoy!' because that's what sailors did in the book she had read. _____ told everyone to get ready to land. She knew that they would have to jump into the water and swim or paddle to the shore.

'I can't swim!' said _____.

'That's all right,' _____ told him. 'The water won't be very deep. _____ and _____ will help you.

The bottom of the boat scraped on the sand and we all began to climb over the side. It was not far to dry land, but _____,

_____ and _____ all managed to get completely soaked when a big wave washed over them as they paddled ashore.

Everyone sat on the sand in the sunshine looking at the island. Tall trees could be seen at the top of the cliff and a river flowed right through the middle of the beach and into the sea.

'Look at those mountains!' called _____, pointing up at the huge, misty hills which towered above everything else.

'I want to climb them,' cried _____, and _____ and _____ said that they did too.

When they had rested for a few minutes, the children set off to explore the island. They decided to split up into small groups and then meet on the beach two hours later.

Fantasy Island, see page 60

Fantasy Island (3)

_____, _____, _____ and _____ said that they would look in the woods for food.

_____ and _____ offered to try to catch some fish, and went off to look for wood to make a fishing rod.

_____ had some string in her pocket to make a line.

_____, _____ and _____ said that they would climb the mountains and would take paper with them from the boat so that they could draw a map of the island.

_____, _____, _____ and _____ went off to gather firewood so that they could build a fire to cook the fish.

'That's if you manage to catch any!' laughed _____.

_____, _____, _____ and _____ said that before they went exploring they would go back on to the boat and drop the anchor so that it would not drift away.

Everyone was excited. The children knew that they could get home safely so long as the boat was all right. Now they wanted to explore the island and look for adventure.

▲ Can you continue the story and write about the children's adventures on the island? You can use the back of this sheet.

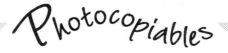

Three wishes (1)

Name _____   **Date** _____

The wood was dark and cool after walking in the sunshine. Ella and Lewis could see shafts of light breaking through the trees. They could hear the noise of tiny animals hiding as they approached.

Soon they came to a small clearing in the woods and they stopped and looked around them. Their parents would be along in a moment. They thought about hiding and giving them a surprise. One of the trees had a large hole in its trunk which one of them would be able to squeeze into, but there would not be room for two. As they looked at the hole in the tree they suddenly realised that the woods had become quiet. The sound of animals and birdsong had gone. Ella and Lewis looked at each other and then at the wood around them. Just as Lewis was about to speak he stopped and gazed at the hole in the tree, his mouth open and his eyes wide.

'What are you two staring at?' The voice was squeaky and it belonged to a little man who had climbed out of the hole in the tree. He was unlike any person they had ever seen before. On his head he wore a green hat with a feather tucked into a band and a rim which came down over his forehead. His eyes were bright and

sparkling and he had a long grey beard which covered the front of his green coat and reached the belt of his brown trousers. He wore black boots and although he looked old enough to be their grandfather he was slightly smaller than the children.

The children were too shocked to move. They went on staring at the little man hardly believing their eyes. 'Will you stop staring at me,' said the man crossly. 'Haven't you ever seen a triwishman before?'

Three wishes, see page 62

Three wishes (2)

At last Ella managed to find her voice. 'What's a triwish watsit?' she asked.

'A triwishman is a person like me who grants three wishes to people. Now, if you will both stop staring at me, tell me three good reasons why I should make your three wishes come true.' The little man sounded grumpy, but his eyes glowed in the way that eyes do when a person is smiling. The children could not tell if he was really smiling because his beard hid his mouth.

'Come on then, you first, Lewis. Yes, I know your name. I've been waiting for you for a long time. Now tell me why I should let you have three wishes, and while he's doing that you had better start thinking too, Ella.'

The children looked at each other and Lewis began to speak.

▲ If you had three wishes, what would you wish for?

1

2

3

▲ Can you finish the story? Imagine that you are Lewis or Ella. You can use the back of this sheet.

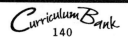

My ideal birthday

Name _____   **Date** _____

7.30 -------- When I wake up the first thing I see will be...

------------ For breakfast I will have...

------------ My presents will be...

------------ I will receive birthday cards from...

------------ For a special treat I will...

------------ For tea I will have...

------------ When it is bedtime I will...

The game of the book, see page 65

A story game: Jack and the Beanstalk

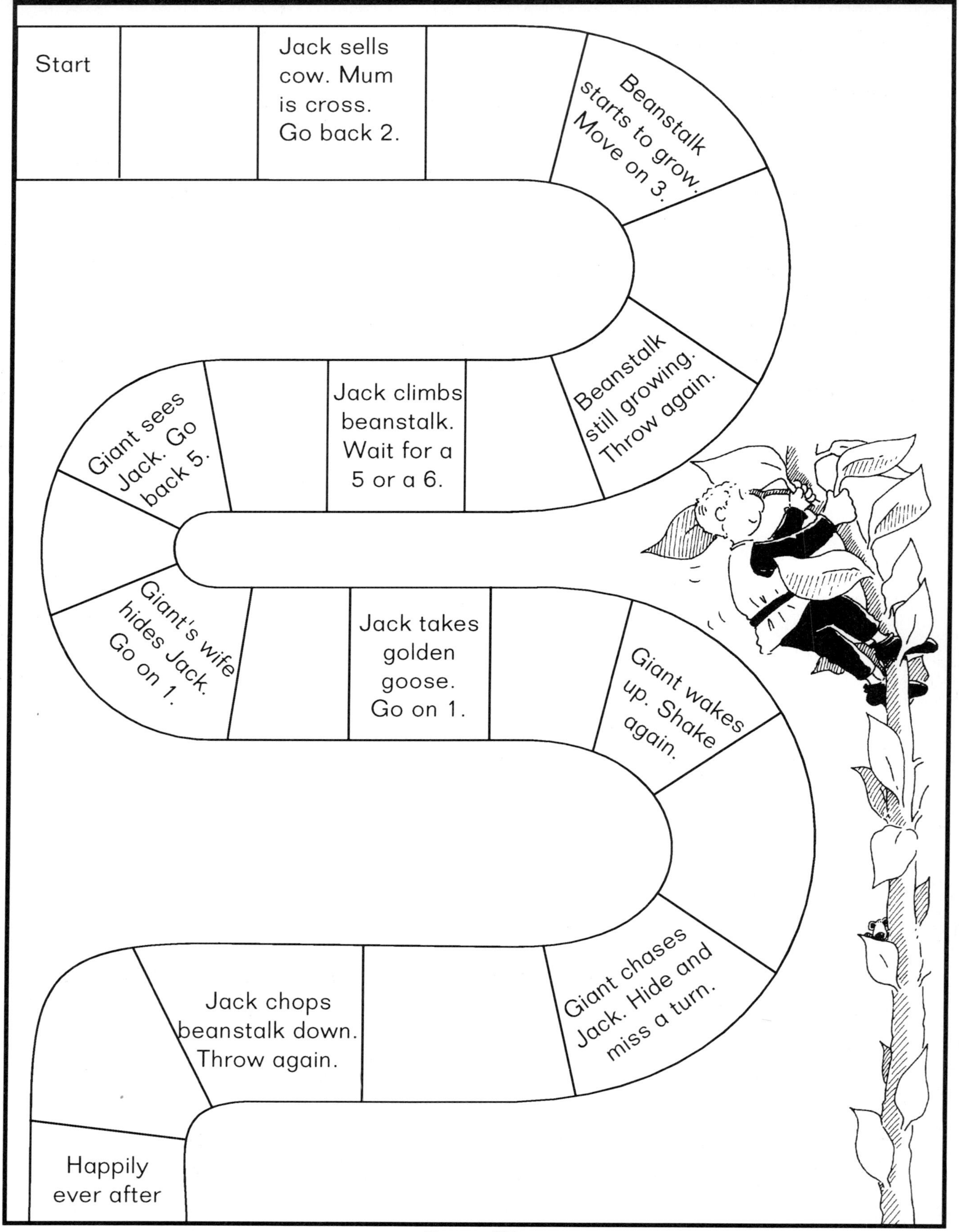

Start

Jack sells cow. Mum is cross. Go back 2.

Beanstalk starts to grow. Move on 3.

Beanstalk still growing. Throw again.

Giant sees Jack. Go back 5.

Jack climbs beanstalk. Wait for a 5 or a 6.

Giant's wife hides Jack. Go on 1.

Jack takes golden goose. Go on 1.

Giant wakes up. Shake again.

Giant chases Jack. Hide and miss a turn.

Jack chops beanstalk down. Throw again.

Happily ever after

The middle of the story, see page 67

The middle of the story

Name _____   **Date** _____

▲ Fill in the space by writing the middle of the story.

One day Tom and Lucy went to visit their gran. She lived in an old, stone house next to a lake. When they arrived, Tom and Lucy found the house was empty. There was a note which said, 'Gone out to catch fish for lunch. I'll be back by ten o'clock.' Lucy looked at her watch. It was already half-past ten.

   The children decided to go out and look for their gran. She was very fit and healthy, but they were afraid that something might have happened to her.

   The boat was empty. They could see Gran's fishing rod in the water. 'Look!' said Tom. He pointed to a tree at the edge of the lake.

   'It's Gran,' cried Lucy. 'Let's go and rescue her!'

   They found Gran holding on to the branches of the tree. Her clothes were wet, but she did not seem at all upset.

   Later, at Gran's house, while they were all drinking cocoa, Gran could not stop laughing as she explained what had happened.

The end of the story, see page 68

The end of the story

▲ Read the story and see if you can write your own ending.

It was cold and dark. Rachel and Alex were tired and hungry. It seemed like days since they had had tea but it was only five hours.

If only they had stayed at home and watched television. Instead they had come with Mum on one of her walks. Mum loved to trudge through mud and up and down hills. The trouble was she was always getting lost. They were always telling her to take a map with her but she always told them that she knew the way.

This time they were really lost. No one remembered ever seeing the hills and valleys they were seeing now. The sun had set long ago and they did not have a torch. The only light came from the Moon. The trees looked like big black monsters against the moonlit sky and the only sound came from the sheep on the hillside.

'I want to go home,' said Alex.

'So do I and I don't ever want to go for a walk again!' Rachel told her mother.

Before Mum had a chance to tell them to stop grumbling they all stopped suddenly and stared.

'What is it?' asked Alex.

'I don't like it,' said Rachel.

'Come on Rachel and Alex. Let's take a closer look,' said Mum firmly.

That's the trouble with Mum, thought the children, she's never afraid of anything. The three of them began to move forward slowly in the darkness. The children gripped their mother's hands tightly and Alex closed his eyes. He only opened them when he heard Mum say, 'Oh my goodness. I've never seen anything like that before!'

▲ What had Mum, Rachel and Alex found?

▲ What do you think might happen next? Can you finish the story?

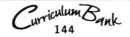

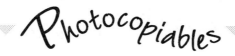

Arranging and completing the story, see page 69

Rearrange and finish the story

▲ This story is jumbled up. Read all of the sentences and then put them into an order that makes sense. Cut the sentences out and arrange them on your table, so that you can read the story. The first sentence is number 2.

1	The dog did not have anyone to live with.
2	Once upon a time there was a little dog.
3	The dog thought that his name was Go Away, because that's what everyone said to him when he went into the town.
4	He thought the cry came from an old, stone house which stood at the end of the street.
5	The dog wandered from place to place looking for food.
6	He decided that he would go and see if he could help.
7	He did not even have a name.
8	One day, the dog was looking for food when he heard a cry.

▲ Now try to write your own ending for the story. What do you think the dog will find in the house? What will happen to the dog? Will the dog find his name?

Picture stories, see page 81

Picture stories (1)

Name _____   Date _____

Picture stories, see page 81

Picture stories (2)

Name _____   Date _____

Police

The hole in the fence, see page 83

The hole in the fence

Name _____   **Date** _____

I was walking around the garden of our new house on the day after we moved in when I noticed that there was a very tall wooden fence at the end of the garden. I did not remember seeing the fence before and I became very curious about what might be behind it.

The wood was old and dark brown and the fence was much too high for me to see over it. Even if someone had lifted me up I would not have been able to see what was on the other side.

I walked up and down the garden next to the fence and I tried to imagine what might be on the other side. It was quiet and the only sounds came from birds singing and distant traffic. The sun shone warmly and the sky was clear and blue. I really wanted to know what was on the other side of the fence. Perhaps there would be children I could play with or a dog I could make friends with. There could be trees to climb or a field to play in.

I had just decided that I would never be able to find out what was on the other side of the fence when I noticed a small gap right in the middle. I looked at it carefully. If I tried hard I thought I might be able to squeeze through the hole and then I would be able to explore.

▲ What do you think happens next? Can you finish the story? Use the back of this sheet.

A Christmas stocking

Name _____   **Date** _____

▲ Glue pictures of presents on to the packages and then write the name of each present.

I went on my holiday

Name _____   **Date** _____

▲ Use the spaces on the suitcases to make notes of the things which people take on their holidays. Write the first thing in number 1, the second in number 2 and so on.

1.

2.

3.

5.

4.

6.

7.

8.

10.

9.

A letter from a visitor, see page 92

A letter from a visitor

Dear Children

I really enjoyed visiting your classroom. I had a good look around before I left last night. It is very quiet when you have all gone home!

I heard you all trying to guess my name. Nobody has got it right yet. Why not write to me and let me know if you have any other ideas?

I would like to know more about you. Would you write and tell me about the things you like to do best, please? What sort of games do you like to play? What do you like to do at school? I like football and I like writing stories.

Do you have a favourite television programme? I really like cartoons and I love to watch Postman Pat.

Please leave a letter for me to find next time I visit your classroom.

Love from

Labelling a bicycle, see page 93

Labelling a bicycle

Name _____   Date _____

light

seat

chain

brake

handlebar

pedal

wheel

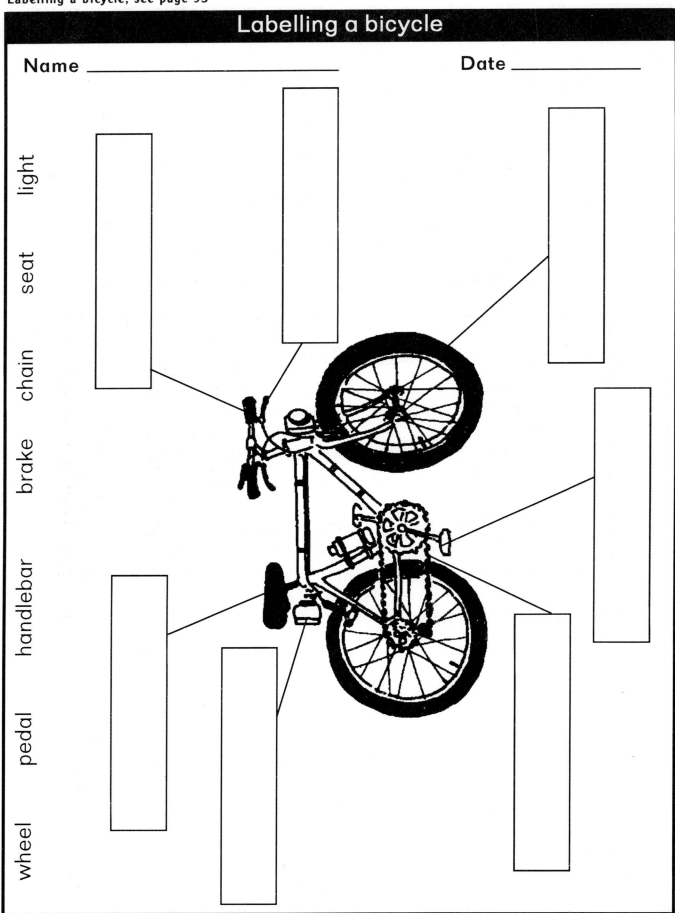

Lost and found

Name _____ **Date** _____

Lost

Small brown and white dog. One ear missing.
Walks with a slight limp. Part of tail missing.
Answers to the name of Lucky.

Please tell Susan Carter at Brook Farm.

Found

Talking bird. Please hurry up and collect it.
It knows some terrible words! Yellow and green
with yellow patch around right eye. Seems to
prefer milk to water. Loves looking in mirror.
Eats anything and everything.

Will sell to pet shop if not claimed by Friday.
Please tell Mrs Black at Rose Cottage.

▲ Can you use the space below to make up your own lost or found
notice?

Lists, see page 96

Lists

Name _____   **Date** _____

▲ Can you write a title for each list and then add more words?

A list of...................   **A list of**...................   **A list of**...............

dog   rose   blue
rabbit   daffodil   yellow

....

....

....

▲ See how many things you can put into each list.

A list of drinks   **A list of clothes**   **A list of toys**
lemonade   hat   doll

....

....

....

....

....

....

....

Photocopiables

Diary of my day

Name _____   Date _____

▲ Fill in the spaces to show what you did at different times of the day.

Before _____ I did these things...

Between _____ and _____ I did these things...

At lunchtime I did these things...

Between lunchtime and _____ I did these things...

Between _____ and _____ I did these things...

The thing I liked doing best today was...

Developing a word bank, see page 102

A word bank

a
about
after
again

b
because
before

c
came
come
could

d
do
does
down

e
each
every

f
first
from

g
give
goes

h
have
help
house

i
inside

j
just

k
know

l
learn
like
little
love

m
many
minute
much

n
name
next
nothing

o
once
one
our

p
people
picture

q
quick
quiet

r
ready
right

s
said
school
should

t
talk
teacher
their
there
through

u
use
used

v
very

w
walk
want
watch
water
what
when
where
who
why
would
write

y
year
you
your

Treasure hunts

Oh where is the treasure
Oh where can it be?
Is it under the floorboards
Or up in a tree?

The first clue's right here
You've only to look.
It's up on a shelf,
But it isn't a book.

The next clue is hidden
Down in the ground –
But here in the classroom
Is where it is found.

Where is the next clue?
It's under a table
It's next to the wall
But it isn't a cable.

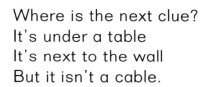

The next clue is flying
Like a bird through the air.
A breeze makes it move
But it's going nowhere.

The last clue is hidden
Behind a small door,
Where a wheel spins around
Never touching the floor.

And the treasure is pleasure
And pleasure is fun,
And it shines in the window
But isn't the sun.

(Answers: ornament, plant pot, skirting board, mobile, pet cage, golden package)

INFORMATION TECHNOLOGY WITHIN WRITING

Main IT Focus

The main emphasis for the development of IT capability within these activities is on communicating information, and in particular on word processing. Indeed most of the activities in this book can involve word processing in some form or other. Where opportunities for IT have not been identified specifically, there may still be basic word-processing tasks that can be undertaken by some or all of the children.

Word processors

It is important that children have the opportunity to originate their work at the computer keyboard, rather than always writing it out longhand and simply using the word processor to make a 'fair copy' for their folder or display purposes. It is often appropriate for children to make their first draft at the keyboard, save it, print it out and then redraft it away from the keyboard, thus giving another child the opportunity to use the computer. They can then return later on to make any changes they have decided upon and format the final copy for printing.

Of course, not every child has to undertake every writing task suggested in the activities. The teacher could organise children to undertake different writing tasks over a term or longer, some using more conventional written methods and others using the computer. This would also provide an opportunity for teachers to provide activities at different levels of IT capability and to discuss with children the relative merits of the use of IT for varying purposes.

During Key Stage 1, pupils will be developing their confidence and competence to use the standard computer keyboard. They should be taught a range of basic keyboard and word-processing skills. These should include learning how to:
▲ understand the layout of the keyboard and where the letter and number keys are found;
▲ use the shift key to type capital letters and characters found on the number keys;
▲ use the delete key to erase words and letters;
▲ use the cursor/arrow keys, or mouse, to position the cursor at the desired position;
▲ use more than a single finger/hand when typing, particularly when knowledge of location of letters is gained;
▲ use the space bar, using the thumb (not the fingers) to press it;
▲ allow the word processor to 'wrap' the text around the end of each line, so there is no need to press the return key at the end of each line;
▲ join text using the delete key;
▲ separate text or create new lines using the return key;
▲ move the cursor to a mistake and correct it, rather than deleting all the text back to the mistake, making the correction and then retyping the deleted text;
▲ print out their completed work, initially with support from the teacher, but eventually on their own.

Children will also need to save their work if they are unable to finish it in one session. They should be taught how to do this on to the hard or floppy disk so that eventually they can do it without teacher assistance. They will then need to be shown how to locate and retrieve their work at a later date.

Young children will take a long time to enter text at the keyboard, so it is important to ensure that the writing tasks are kept short and that where possible there is other support available to teach, and assist the child's development. If parents or other adults are available they can often be used in this way, provided they have the relevant skills, and know when to intervene. Alternatively, they can be used for scribing for longer tasks, typing in the children's work and then going through it with them to edit and alter it.

Some of the suggested activities use word-processed files created in advance by the teacher. Such activities reduce the necessity for text entry and can enable children to concentrate on a new language concept or skill, or on the more sophisticated word-processing commands of editing, organising and presenting their work for an audience. When such files are created it is important to make sure that a backup is kept and where possible the 'master' file is locked against accidental overwriting when children save their amended version of the file.

For many of the writing tasks children can use the standard page format that is presented to them when the software is started. However, for more complex tasks the teacher may wish to set up the page layout before the children start and save it, for example, as a birthday card layout. Children can then start with this basic menu layout and then begin to alter it if they need to.

Multimedia authoring software

This software is a relatively recent addition for most schools, but is proving to be a very versatile and powerful medium. It combines many of the features of a word processor or desktop publishing package but its main difference is that the pages of a child's work can be linked together. The software is able to handle a range of different information including text, pictures from art and drawing packages and digitised pictures from scanned images. Work with authoring packages is best undertaken as part of a longer project, with children working in groups. A class presentation can be split among several groups, with each group preparing the text and pictures for their section and deciding how the pages are to be laid out and linked. Children will need to be taught how to create frames, alter text styles, add colours, import graphics and sound files from other disks and make the links between pages.

IT links

The grids on this page relate the activities in this book to specific areas of IT and to relevant software resources. Activities are referenced by page number, and bold page numbers indicate activities which have expanded IT content. The software listed is a selection of programs generally available to primary schools, and is not intended as a recommended list.

AREA OF IT	SOFTWARE	ACTIVITIES (PAGE NOS.)		
		CHAPTER 1	**CHAPTER 2**	**CHAPTER 3**
Communicating information	Word processor	17, 18, 19, 20, 23, 24, 26, 28, 29, 30, 34, 36, **37**, 38, 40, 41, 42	48, 51, 54, 55, 57, 63, **64**, 65, 67, 68, 69, 71, 73, 75, 76, 77, 78, 79, 80	89, 92, 93, 95, 96, 97, 98, 99, 100, 105, 106, 108
Communicating information	Concept keyboard	17, 18, 28	**51**, 75, 80	
Communicating information	Art/Drawing	26, 29, 38	48, 54, 60, 65, 78	**86**, 91, 101
Communicating information	DTP		**62**, 64	86, 98, 100
Communicating information	Framework	18, 38	48	
Communicating information	Authoring	29	**76**, 82	108
Communicating information	e-mail		52	**106**
Information handling	CD-ROM		58	

SOFTWARE TYPE	BBC/MASTER	RISCOS	NIMBUS/186	WINDOWS	MACINTOSH
Word processor	Stylus Folio Prompt/Writer	Phases Pendown Desk Top Folio	All Write Write On	My Word Kid Works 2 Creative Writer	Kid Works 2 EasyWorks Creative Writer
DTP	Front Page Extra	Desk Top Folio 1st Page	Front Page Extra NewSPAper	Creative Writer NewSPAper	Creative Writer
Framework		My World		My World	
Art Package	Picture Builder	1st Paint Kid Pix Splash	Picture Builder	Colour Magic Kid Pix 2	Kid Pix 2
Database	Our Facts Grass Pigeonhole Datashow	DataSweet Find IT	Our Facts Datashow	Sparks ClarisWorks Information Workshop	ClarisWorks EasyWorks

	MATHS	SCIENCE	HISTORY	GEOGRAPHY	D & T	IT	ART	MUSIC	RE
LANGUAGE STUDY		Discussing pets. Describing animals. Devising questions for a topic.	Devising questions for a topic.	Planning and drawing a picture of a street. Devising questions for a topic.	Children making books about themselves. Making a set of word cards.	Use of word processor for planning and revising work and for text manipulation.	Designing packaging for different products.		Discussing people who are helpful in day-to-day life.
IMAGINATIVE WRITING	Writing timetables for ideal birthdays.	Discussing the weather and seasons. Examining leaves and their different features.		Designing a map of a 'fantasy island'.	Designing fantastic machines. Making a scarecrow. Constructing a board game. Designing an ideal car.	As above.	Drawing monsters. Studying famous paintings.	Tape-recording sounds heard around the school.	Writing prayers for a harvest festival.
NON-FICTION WRITING	Looking at the prices of items in a class shop.	Observation work.	Reading diary extracts from historical figures.		Making Christmas stockings. Making birthday cards.	As above.	Choosing pictures of party food. Designing party invitations.	Listening to music associated with Christmas.	Discussing the meaning of Christmas.